Contents

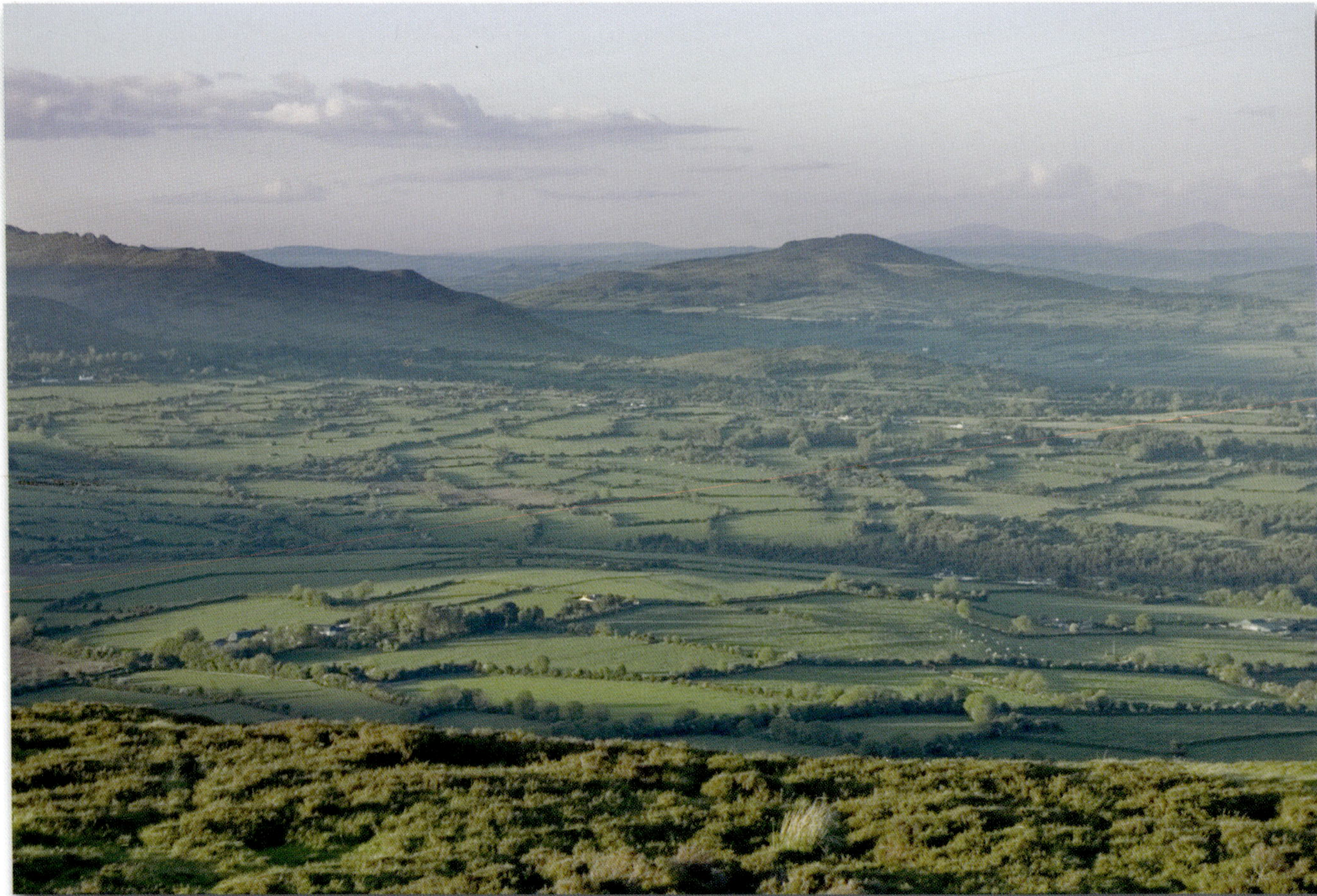

View from Holy Year Cross, Kilrossanty

Introduction

Poet, Tom Power, has brought delight and gladness to the people of Waterford over many years with his poems and songs, commemorating the unfolding events and the lives of those with whom he lives. He is carrying on the Irish bardic tradition, which kept the spirit of the nation alive during times of hunger and tribulation. His poems are the poetry of the people and the county he loves so well. He does not write for the abstract world market but expresses the thoughts and dreams of his neighbours and friends. These poems are heart felt expressions of his love for his native place. Those who know him will know that the sentiments of his poems are only a written manifestation of the great works of charity he does on a daily basis.

The beauty of the poems is then enhanced by the magnificent collection of stunning photographs by Jackie Elger, who is now a resident of the Comeraghs. She has been captivated by the beauty that surrounds her in her mountain home; fascinated by the ever changing light of the landscape; the weather and seasons and is eager to preserve in images the heritage of the countryside.

This anthology has poems and pictures that cover the county of Waterford, which is known locally as 'The Déise County', (the Déisi were an ancient tribe of native Gaelic people who inhabited the area). From Kill to Kilmacthomas; Dunmore East to Dungarvan and from the Comeraghs to the Copper Coast, there is something for everyone in this collection.

This is a book for all to enjoy, at home and abroad and will grace the bookshelves and coffee tables of those who love poetry and who love Waterford.

Seán Murphy 2007
Waterford author and historian.

Bonmahon's Famous Whale

I met with Johnny Fleming, 'twas he first told me the tale,
Of lovely famed Bonmahon and its sixty-three foot whale;
Bonmahon, steeped in history, known for its copper ore,
Awoke one Sunday morning to find this monster on its shore.
Young Colin Dwan (Patsy's son) went searching for driftwood,
When he came to Trá na Lica in amazement there he stood;
The sight that was before him, he couldn't believe his eyes,
The monster from the deep, my God he was some size;
He ran to tell his parents, the news spread from West to East,
The people came from everywhere to view this mighty beast.

The cliffs were thronged with people; they came from Cork and Donegal,
From Dublin and from Belfast, in cars both big and small,
Down the cliffs they climbed at risk of life and limb,
They didn't see the danger; they just had to get to him;
They came to take his photograph for papers and T.V.,
Bonmahon again was famous, just like it used to be.
But also came the scavengers, like vultures to the scene;
They came and watched and waited, to see what they could steal,
The whale to them meant nothing, a quick way to make a pound,
Anywhere there's easy picking, 'tis there the jackals are found.

A Fin whale they said it was, the type that now is rare,
For years they have been hunted, but no one seems to care;
They traveled through the oceans; their kingdom is the deep,
But now in quiet Bonmahon, this one sleeps his final sleep.
There he lies quite helpless, an oddity for all to view,
But when he swam the oceans, he could break a boat in two,
His strength a thing to wonder, his weight near seventy ton,
Now by man and modern methods, they're killed off one by one;
And soon, just like the Dodo, they will be all extinct,
I hope that's not the last one but by God it makes you think.

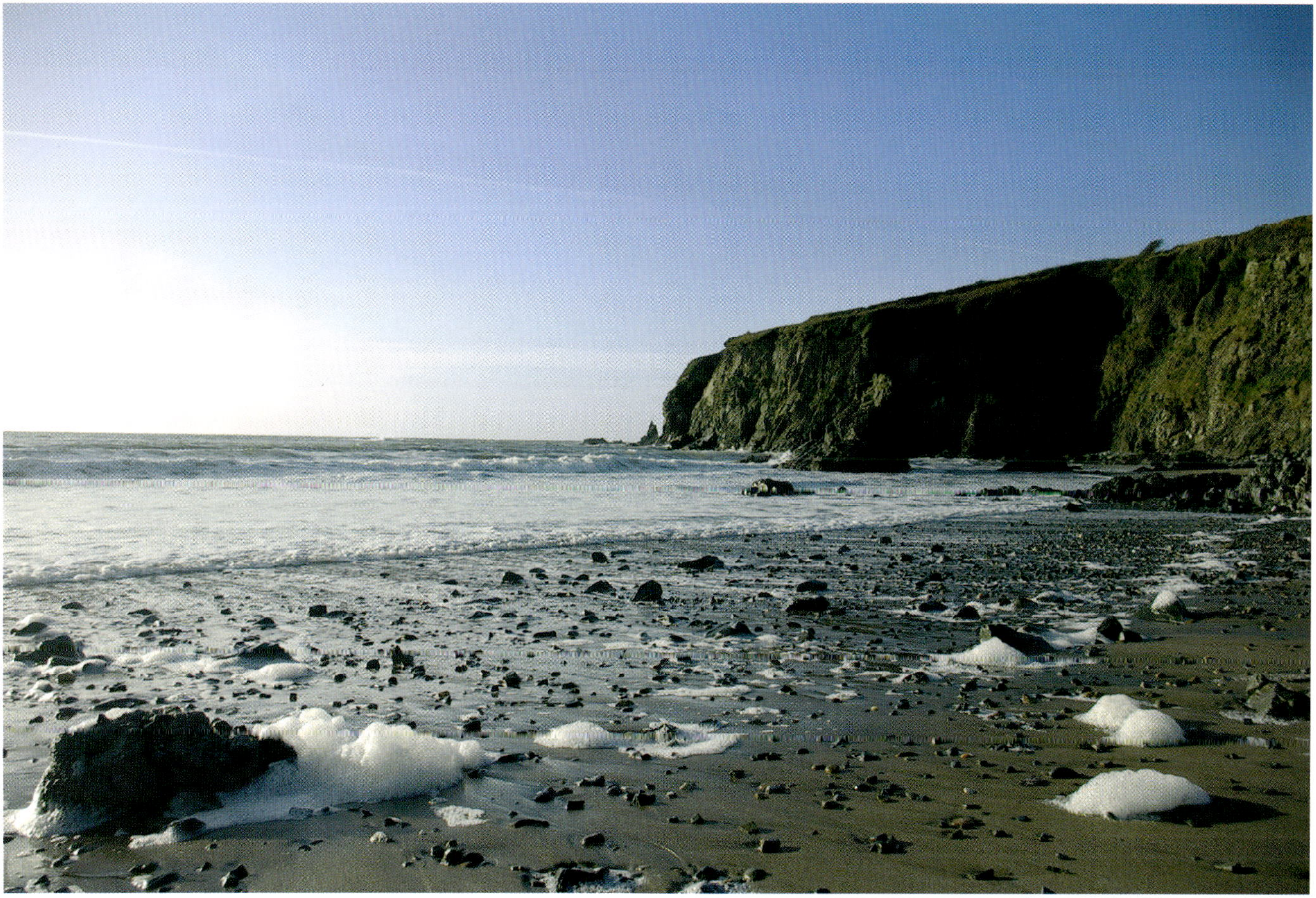

Bonmahon Beach, on the Copper Coast

The Legend of William Crotty

There's a cave up in the Comeraghs near a lake that's deep and cold,
It was the home of William Crotty, that highwayman so bold;
From here he'd travel down to the Dungarvan / Carrick Road,
And he would wait for travellers and relieve them of their load.
"Halt! Stand and deliver", he would shout out loud and clear,
As he robbed them of their riches they stood trembling with fear.
Then he'd jump upon his horse and make his getaway with speed,
And the money that was taken, he would give to those in need.
A gallant man on a horse of white, two pistols by his side,
He robbed the rich to save the poor; he was their hope and pride.

He roamed around the county from Rathgormack to Tramore,
And he was always welcomed at every poor man's door;
The law tried hard to capture him, they chased with gun and hound,
But they couldn't get near him, his hideout couldn't be found.
The bravest man, the fastest horse, the county ever knew,
And to confuse those in pursuit, he'd turn the horse's shoe;
They thought he was going to town when they found fresh made track,
But Crotty wasn't going to, but leaving old Kilmac';
And high upon the Comeraghs, with a view down to the sea,
Man and horse would rest awhile, away from company.

To Kilmacthomas he would travel and mingle at the fair,
He felt safe among them; he had some good friends there;
He'd have a drink with David Norris, he was Crotty's trusted friend,
But David Norris' wife would bring Crotty to his end.
At a place called Shanakill, there lived a man named Hearn,
He talked to Mrs Norris to see what he could learn;
He bribed her to tell him the place of Crotty's cave,
And told her that in doing so, her husband she could save.
She travelled up the mountains with Hearn by her side,
And pointed to a cave and said "there, that's Crotty hide."
A week then passed and she met Hearn and said 'the bird is in the nest',
Hearn went and got his pistols and climbed up to make arrest.

He shouted out "William, a friend has come to call",
Crotty then climbed out and was struck by a small lead ball;
Though he was badly wounded, he was able to get away,
He made his way to Norris, he was there the following day.
Mrs Norris went to Hearn, said "Crotty's at our place,
He is weak and wounded; you shot hit him in the face."
Hearn ran to Norris', sneaked up without a noise,
Busted in the door and took Crotty by surprise;
Saying "Crotty, I arrest you in the name of the Crown,
And I'm going to take you to jail in Waterford town."

They tried young William Crotty, "you are guilty" they said,
The judge passed the sentence: "you will hang until you're dead";
Crotty faced the hangman; he stood tall and brave,
And when they slipped the bolt, he went a hero to the grave.
If you're ever on the mountain when the mist is coming down,
And all is calm and silent and you can't hear a sound;
You gaze into the mist, at shadows big and small,
And one of them reminds you of a horse and man so tall;
Don't get too frightened if that shadow seems to sigh,
It might be William Crotty as he goes riding by.

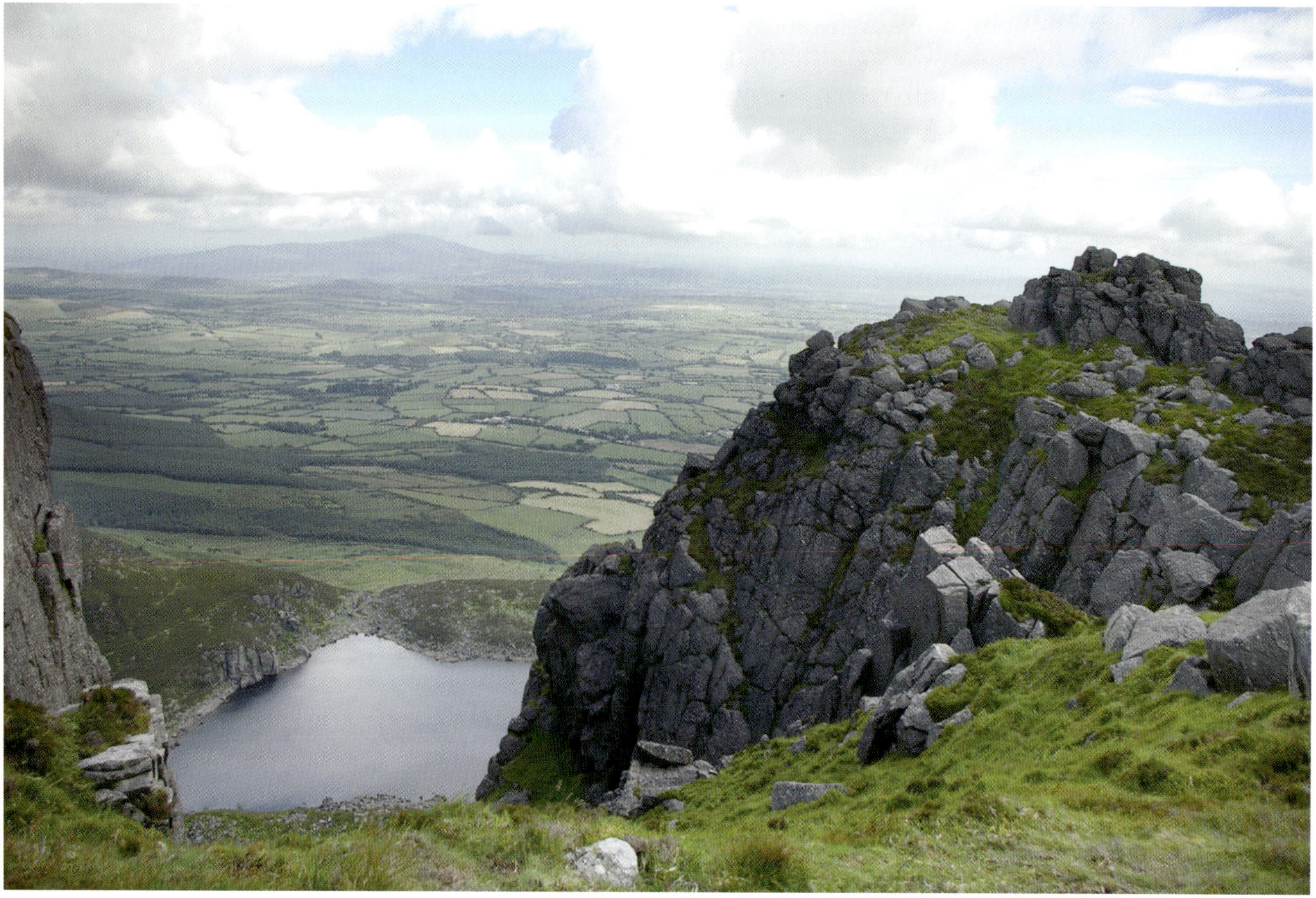

Crotty's Rock and Lake, Comeragh Mountains

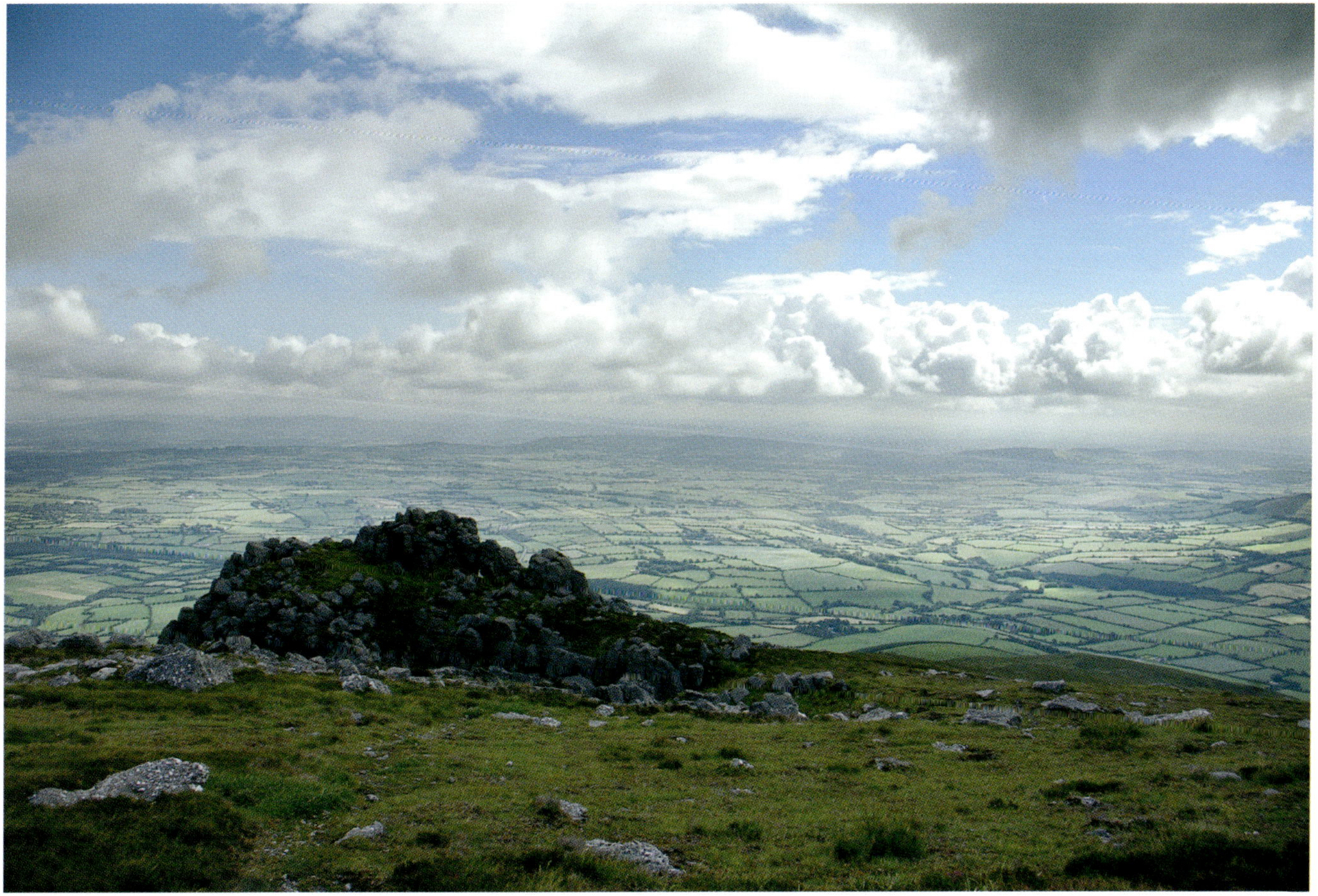

Crotty's Rock, Comeragh Mountains

The Storm

Beneath my boat the sea it gets a little rough
I turn to view my catch; I think I've caught enough;
I haul my line and head by boat back in,
As the storm clouds gather, the day grows dim.
My boat now tied and safe by a sheltered pier,
The wind now rising, the storm is near;
Soon powerful waves will come rolling in and crash against the cliffs,
White spray carried on the wind brings the taste of salt to my lips.
Dark clouds, driven by a south west wind scurry across the sky,
I can hear the call of the seagulls as they circle low and high;
At the base of the sea battered cliffs a white belt of foam,
The wind rising to a high pitched scream, then dropping to a lonesome moan.
Yesterday this sea so calm to me gave forth its wealth,
Now sea and wind combine to form a view of nature's strength.
White capped waves break and crash with a mighty roar,
Stones roll noisily over stones; the returning waves tear them from the shore;
The sea, now a swirling mass of foam and wind-swept spray,
Stooped against the wind, across this storm bashed beach I make my way.
Now the rain falls with a tang of salt rolls down my face,
I turn and make for home, a dry and safer place;
My house so warm and dry, a shelter from the howling wind and rain,
Inside a warm fire, flames drawn up the chimney by the gale;
In the distance I can hear the mighty sea,
Tomorrow its anger spent it will be once more a friend to me.

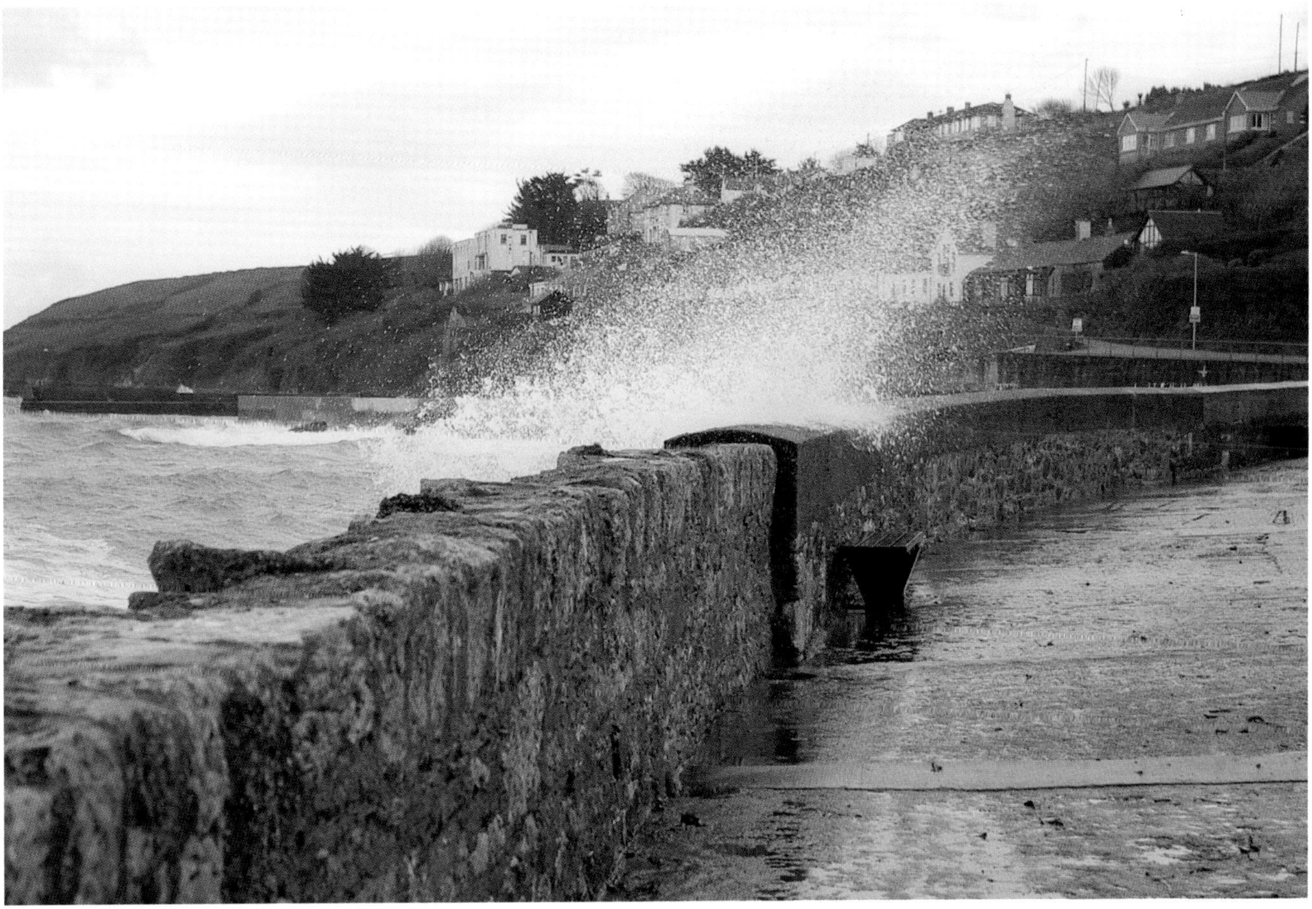

Ardmore

A Bar Stool in Boston

Sitting on a bar stool in Boston my friend and I drinking some beer,
Talking of our home back in Waterford and friends and places so dear;
He was from old Ballybricken a city man right to the core,
And he spoke of his childhood in Waterford and train trips out to Tramore.
I was brought up in the county, a countryman bred, born and reared;
We sit on a bar stool in Boston and boyhood memories compared,
In my mind I could vision the Comeraghs wrapped in a winter blanket of white,
Proudly standing watch over Waterford and a guardian by day and by night.
Green valleys, clear rivers, summer days by the sea,
Those scenes of my childhood, all came back to me.
He then spoke of his city, historical, ancient and new,
And the good times that he had there with boyhood friends he once knew;
He'd love to ramble down town and window shop all of the stores,
Or walk along the quay in the evening and see ships sail in from foreign shores.

I then recalled old Dungarven, strolling around Grattan Square,
Or sit on a seat in the harbour and breathe in the healthy sea air.
Where is the best scenery in Ireland? I will tell you and this is no boast,
If you want the best scenery in Ireland then travel the famed Copper Coast.
So we sat on a barstool in Boston remembering old friends and past times,
I turned and asked him a question, "when will we repeat fifty nine?"
I mentioned Joe Harney and Cheasty, county men both through and through;
Brave, stouthearted and skillful proud of the white and the blue.
He said he knew Frankie Walsh; Seamus Power was his friend way back then;
So we sat on a barstool in Boston and drank a toast to famed Waterford men.
The barman brought us back to the present saying "its time now drink up your beer,"
And as we got off our barstool in Boston I wondered why we are still there,
Faraway over the ocean there's a small piece of heaven on earth;
Its Waterford city and county, the Déise, the place of my birth.

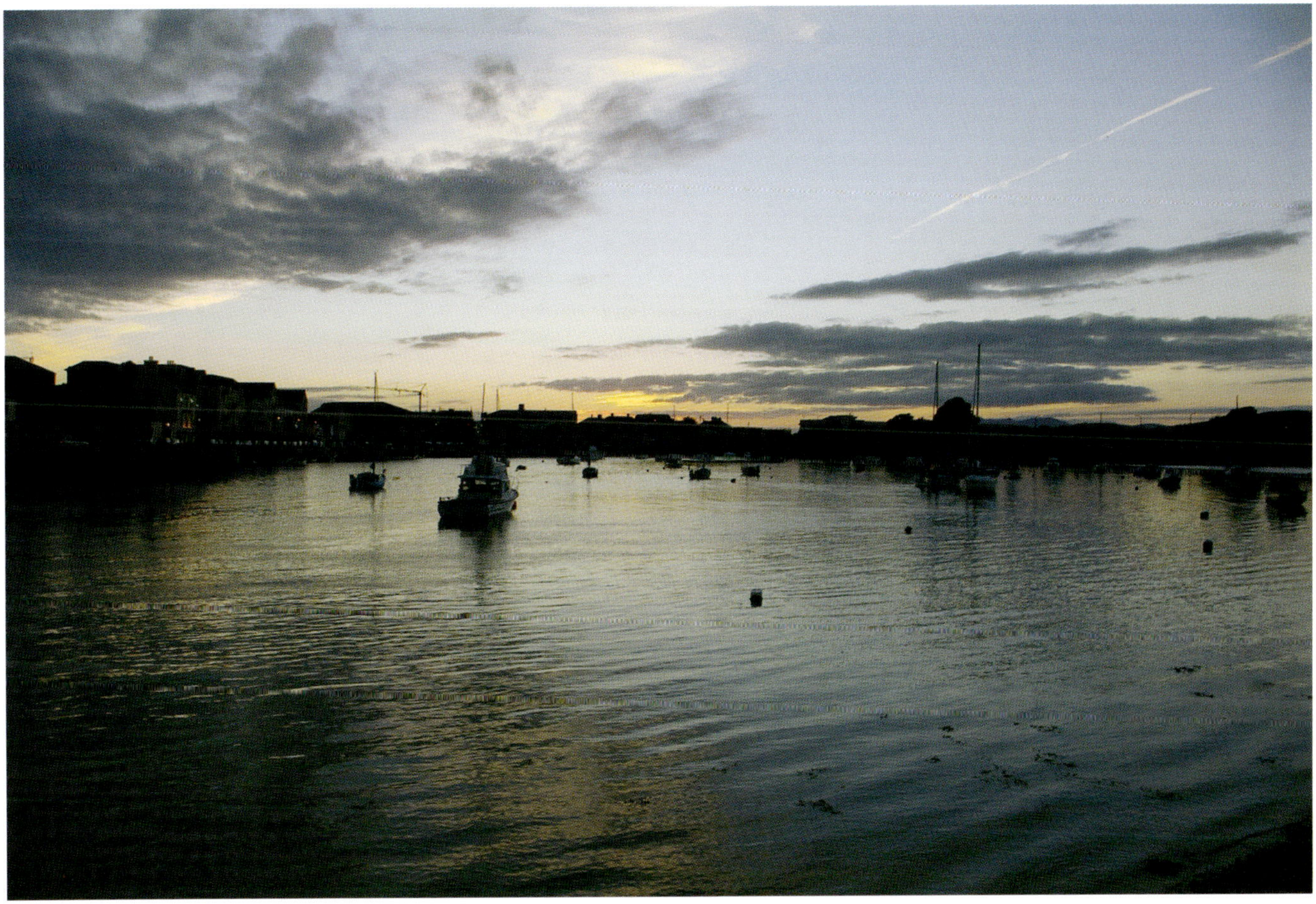

Dungarvan Harbour

A Council Man Remembers

Today is my last day working; I've been pensioned off at last,
But I'd like to tell you all the way it was back there in the past;
I've been a Council man for forty years or more,
Every day at seven I'd be heading out the door.
Up at six each morning, the fire was burning bright,
Sure you know we had no gas then or no electric light.
The flickering light of a candle threw shadows around the room,
I'd sit and eat my breakfast in the early morning gloom;
I'd have an egg if I was lucky and some home-made bread,
Made in the old ovenpot, 'twas the best I've always said.

Then I'd get my tommy can and hang it on the bike,
The shovel on the crossbar, I had it bound up tight;
I'd swing up on the saddle and head off with my load,
The tyres would leave their mark in the grey frost on the road.
Ten miles or more to travel before my work would start,
Through the early morning silence now and then a dog would bark.
I'd meet up with the other lads, John, Pat and Mike,
All day long we'd cut and clean along those dreary dykes,
On the quiet country roads clearing blocked-up drains,
And you knew the friendly houses where to shelter from the rain.

Then sometimes to the quarry, to break and shovel stone,
The east wind blowing around you would chill you to the bone;
But then would come the summer, the days were fine and long,
The birds were whistling loudly, the cuckoo sings his song
Spreading dust along the road out of a horse's car,
And wondering come the weekend could you afford a jar.
The scholars coming home from school would stop and have a chat,
They'd gather round the horse and give his head a pat;
You would travel round the county when you were a Council man,
And at times you had to sleep in a cold and draughty van.

The tommy cans were boiled up, time for a rest and joke,
Sit on the ground; drink your tea, strong with the taste of smoke,
Have a game of pitching, throwing pennies in the can,
And arguing of politics and who's the better man.
All day long you worked from early morn till night,
Your friends would share a fag or maybe fill your pipe.
The Council men are scarce now, machines are in their place,
But the roads around the county are all is some disgrace;
I never saw such potholes and fences are all wild,
Oh, God, be with the old ways, the old shovel, hook and scythe.

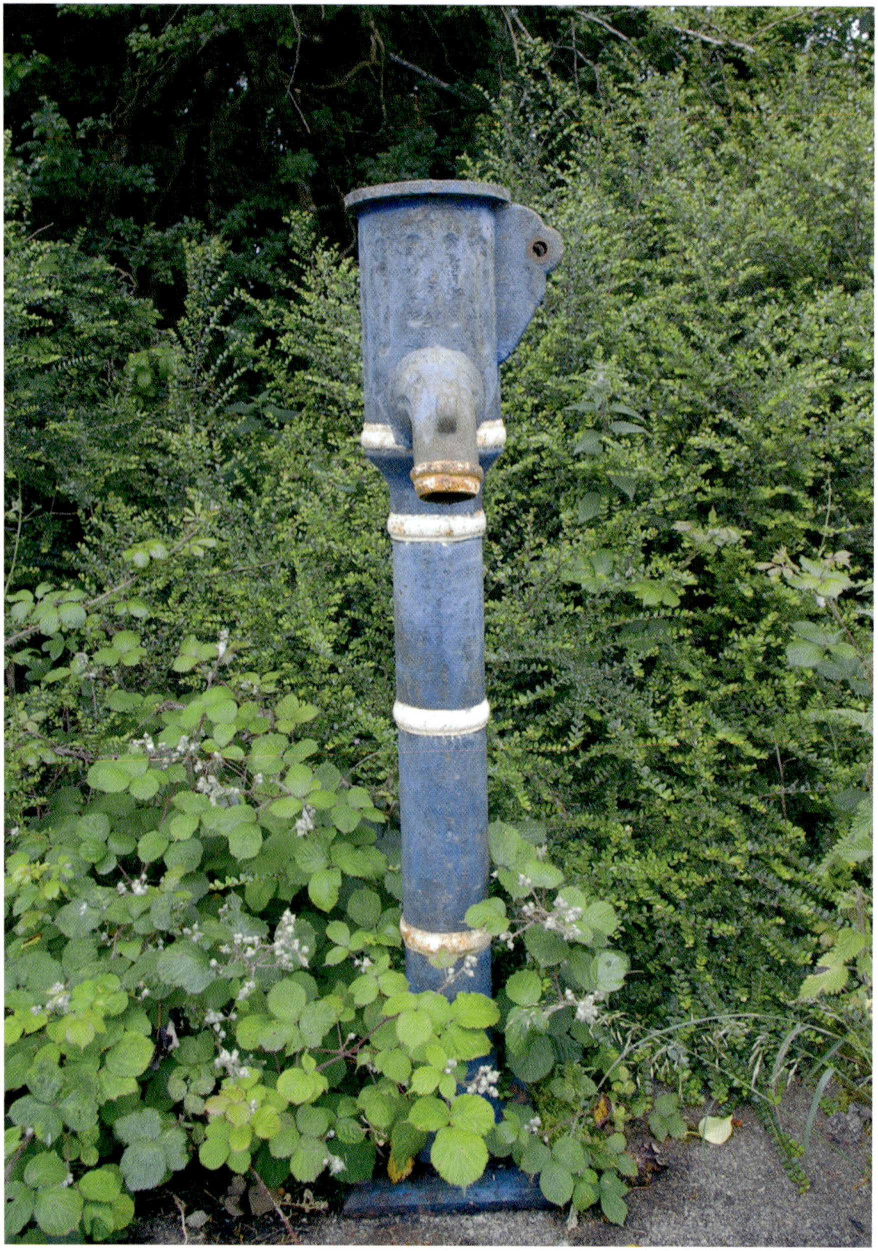

'Water Pump', Kilmacthomas

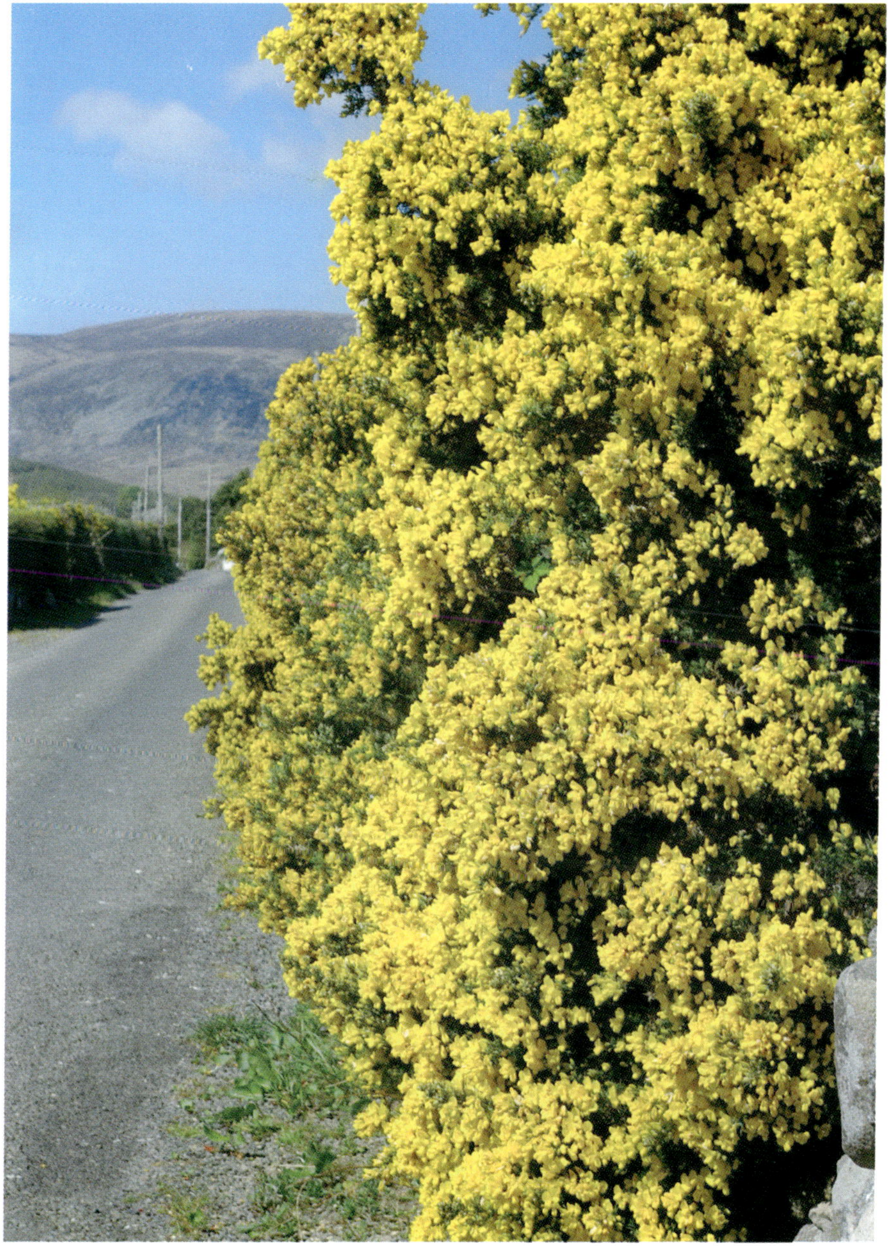

'Summer Gorse', Crough

A Country Sunday

I walked out this morning, the countryside to see,
The sun was shining all around it, warming the world and me;
The green grass it was growing and this I'll have you know,
I heard the trout stream laughing, I stopped to watch it flow.
The birds I heard them singing, they were flying all around,
I saw the cattle grazing, their heads bent to the ground;
The rabbits they were playing, they skipped about the glen,
They stopped to watch as I went by, then hopped and skipped again.

CHORUS
Through a country Sunday I slowly made my way,
Walking out with nature, this lovely sunny day;
Blue skies overhead, green grass beneath my feet,
And all of God's creatures are there for me to meet.

The sheep were like large mushrooms, white spots against the green,
A kestrel hovered overhead, then dived on something he had seen;
The wild flowers they were blooming, I could see them everywhere,
I saw a pheasant flying, a flash of colour through the air.
The hawthorns were in blossom all through the countryside,
I saw a fox go running in search of a place to hide;
I watched the sun rise slowly up in a cloudless sky,
I stood alone with nature, no happier man then I.
CHORUS
The furze upon the hillside were a brilliant green and gold,
I gazed upon their beauty and heard their buds unfold;
I sat upon the old bridge and watched God's work of art,
To be out among this beauty, such gladness filled my heart.
I had shared some time with nature in those fields around my home,
And I know that I'll return there no matter where I roam;
For this is where my heart is and where I want to be,
Just walking along with nature and all nature's things to see.
CHORUS

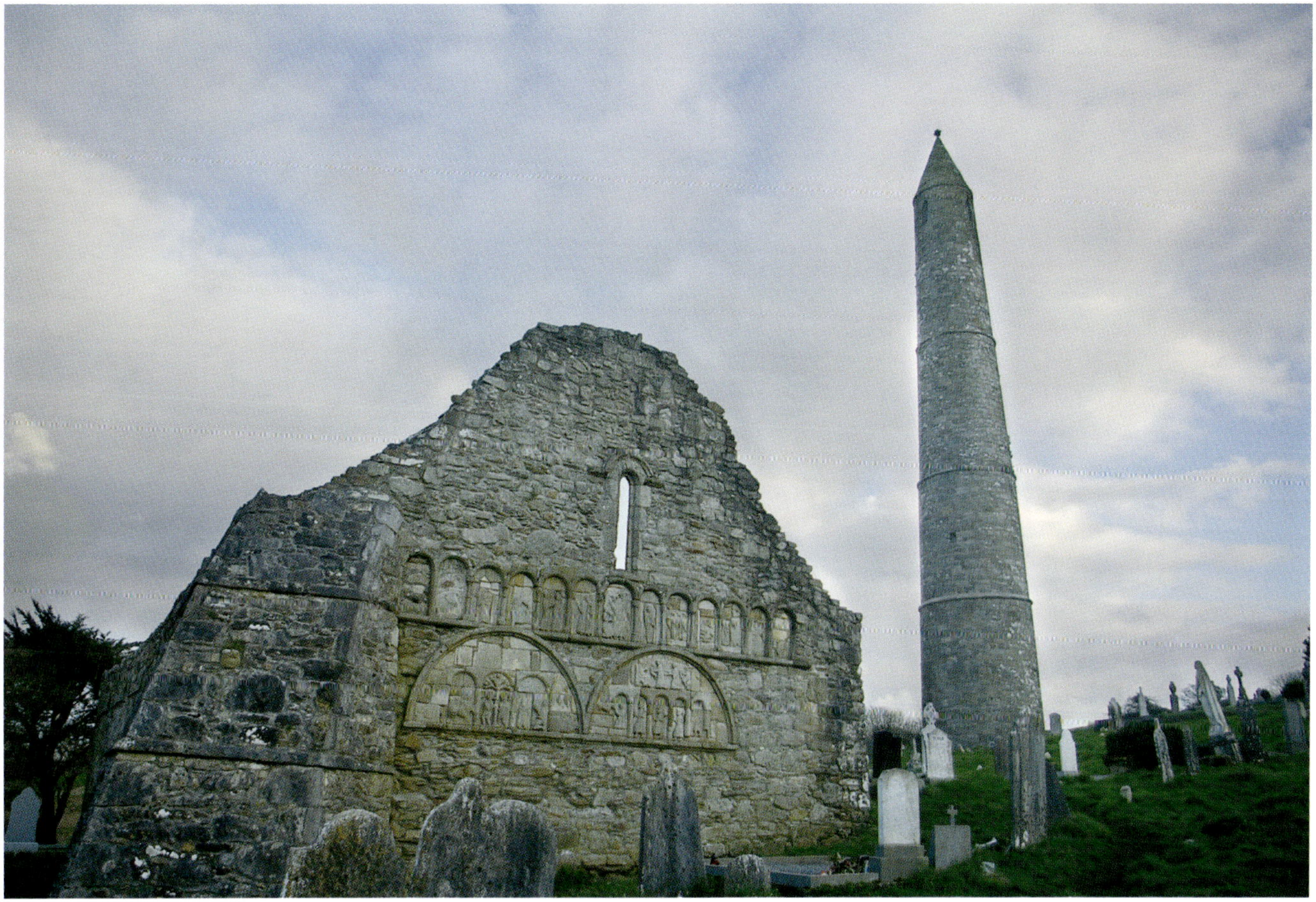

Church and Round Tower, Ardmore

A Christmas Wish

Christmas Eve I stood on a hill,
The night was calm, cold and still;
The stars were shining, oh so bright,
On this very special holy night.
I stood there looking all around,
All was silent – not a sound;
And in the valley down below,
From every window a lovely glow.

A Christmas candle shining clear,
To tell the world that Christ is here;
A guiding light for you and I,
To show the way as we go by.
For in this world that's often dark,
It's nice to see the smallest spark;
And from that spark a light may spread,
To show the road that we must tread.

Down city street and country lane,
To midnight Mass the people came,
To celebrate the birth of Christ,
And pray to God in a united voice.
Help us Christ you are our saviour,
To live in peace as friend and neighbour,
And help us in the coming year,
To rid the world of hate and fear.

Another year has come and gone,
In this world of right and wrong.
Injustice, hunger and constant strife,
Are what some people get from life.
While other people have no care,
They own the world but they won't share,
While millions of people die from hunger,
Greed is tearing this world asunder.

Guns and bombs do what they can,
Man tries hard to destroy man,
And when it's over what will be here,
A burnt-out world and polluted air.
So when we kneel this Christmas day,
All creeds together I beg you pray,
To help our leaders do what's right,
And follow with faith, God's guiding light.

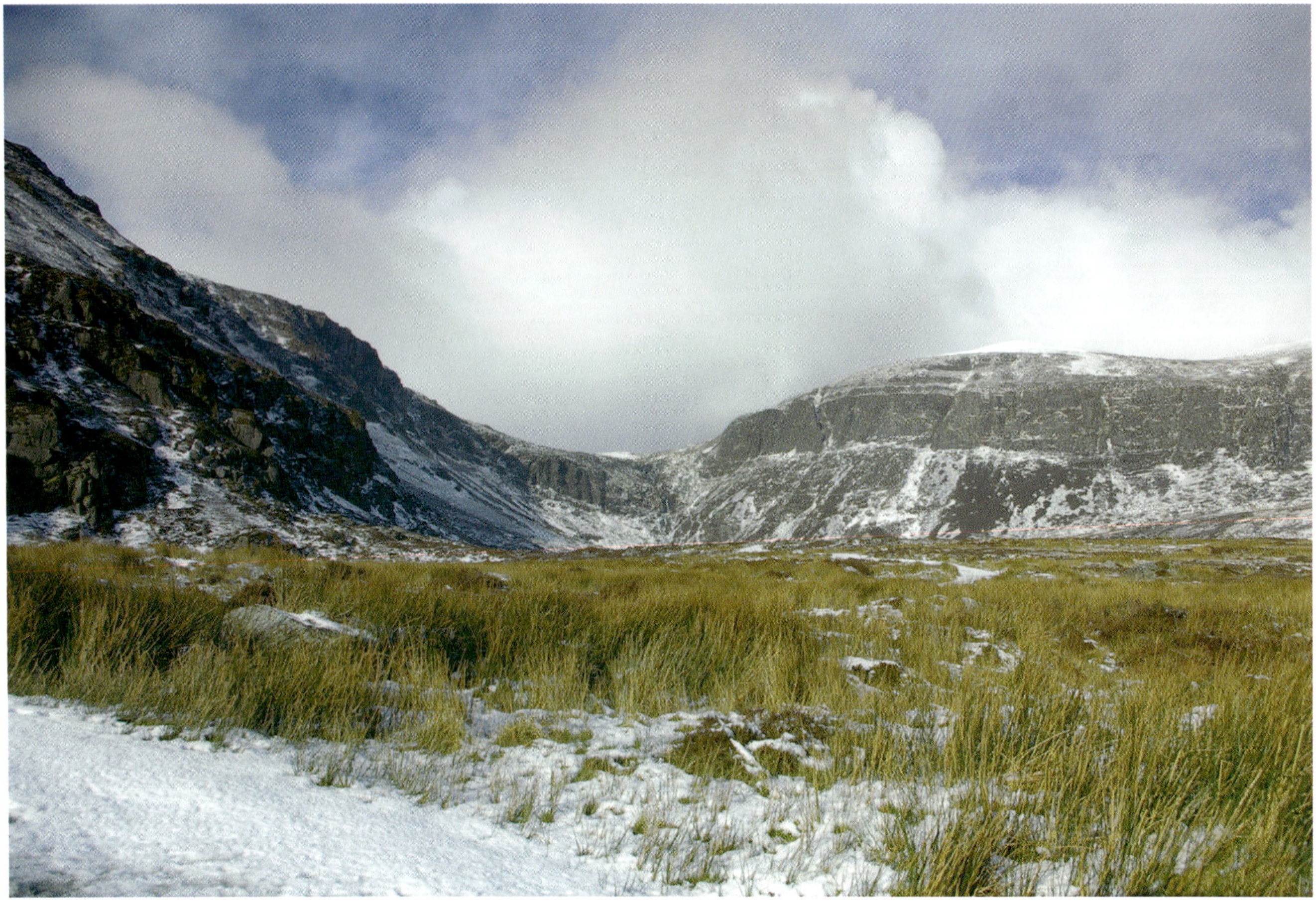

Mahon Falls, Comeragh Mountains

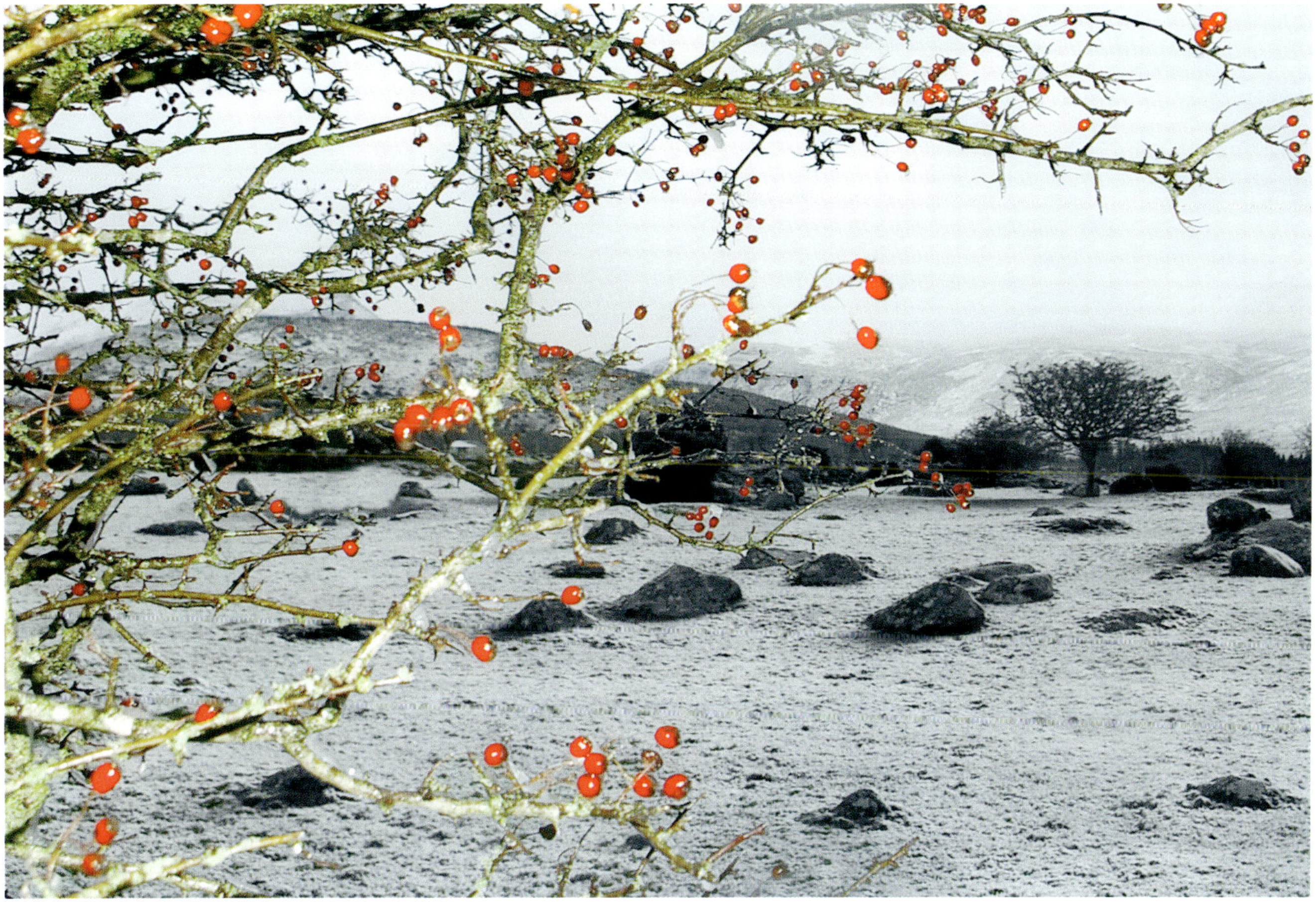

'Winter Hawthorn', Crough

A New Beginning

Daffodils and primroses heat in the sun,
The world is awaking, springtime has come;
The winter is behind us, summer to the fore,
Birds, all are singing and nesting once more.
Buds on the trees, the fields fresh and green,
Darkness defeated, light rules supreme.
Everywhere you look, life pours from the ground,
The laughter of spring can be heard all round.

New hope comes to all, this time of the year,
And belief in the future now that Easter is here;
Spring and Easter, Easter and spring,
To a stagnant world a new life they bring.
A new beginning, an exit from despair,
Christ has saved us, so give thanks in prayer.
We are born, we live and die, but we are not lost,
Because God sent his son to die on the cross.

Good Friday he died on Mount Calvary,
He gave up his life so we could be free;
When they went to the tomb on that first Easter morn,
They found that Christ had overcome the cross and the thorn.
Easter has come and mankind is saved,
Jesus the Saviour has risen from the grave;
The tomb it is empty, he walks with the living,
To all mankind a new life he has given.

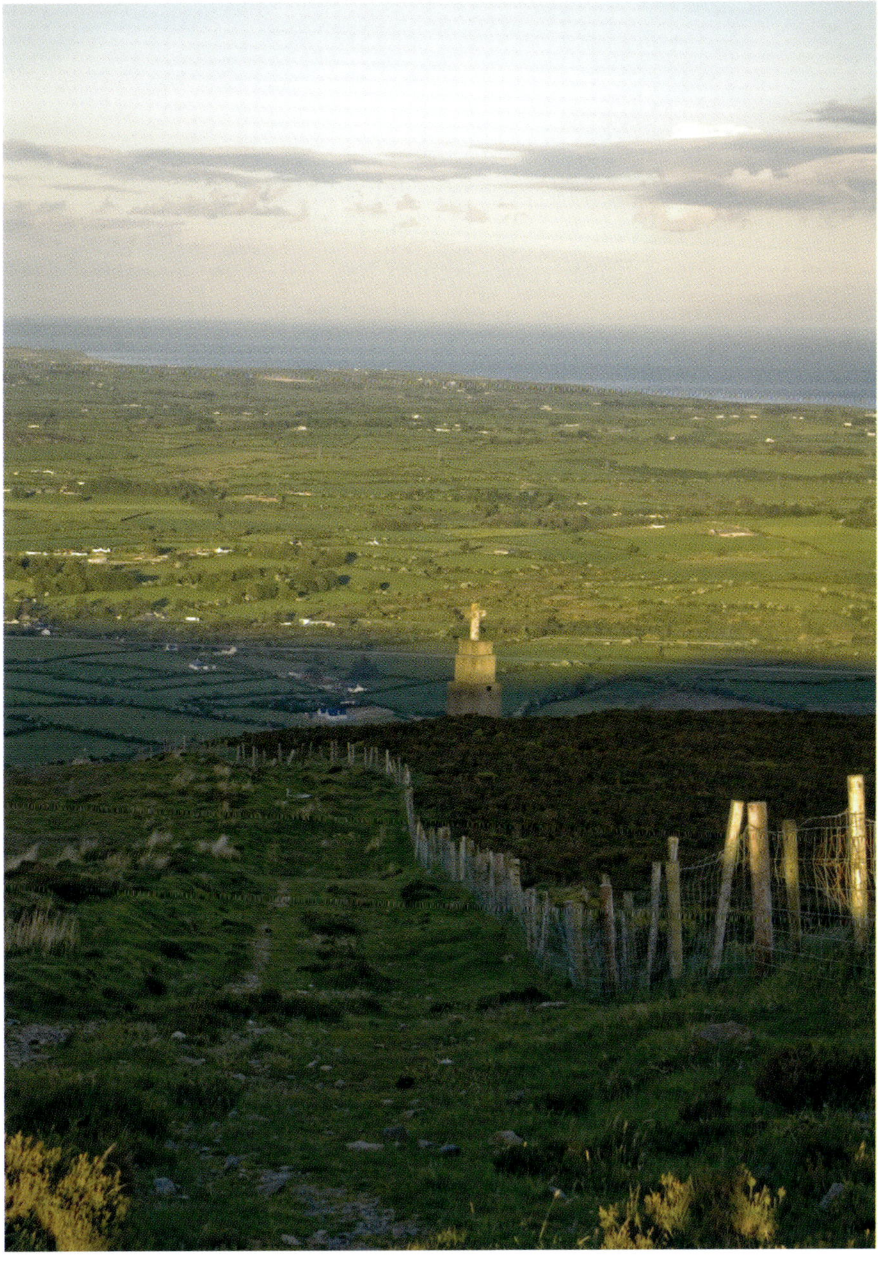

Holy Year Cross, Kilrossanty

Another Place – Another Time

In the foothills of the Comeraghs, far away from grief and pain,
Is the parish of Kilrossanty, nourished by the sun and rain;
There in the little churchyard the Keating brothers rest,
They freely gave their lives for the down-trodden and oppressed.
They fought proudly for their country and bravely they died,
As thousands died before them, to restore their country's pride.
In the year of thirty-nine when the war clouds rolled again,
The call to arms was answered by brave young Irish men;
The thunder of the tyrant could be heard across the sea,
And other little nations were fighting to be free.

Hitler marched across Europe with his Nazis flags unfurled,
To him we all were weaklings and had no place in the world;
To the concentration camps and gas chambers, Jews like cattle driven,
Experiments and torture, no mercy they were given.
Hitler and his henchmen brought Europe to its knees,
From Poland to France the jackboot marched with ease.
Mass graves and executions were the order of the day,
And priceless works of art, for the future stored away,
But God smiles on the merciful, evil will be overcome,
The Allies gained a victory, the Nazis on the run.

Around the world they scattered with their blood-stained treasure,
To hide in lonesome mansions and enjoy their selfish pleasure;
Rembrants and Van Goghs, chandeliers of silver and gold,
Surely they must haunt them and make their blood run cold.
As they sit and gaze upon them in the shadows of the night,
Can they hear the screams of the children they battered with their might?
Can they see the mass graves and the bodies lying there?
Can they smell the rotten corpses and stench of gas in the air?
Could we ever pass a sentence befitting such a crime,
Let God be the judge, another place, another time.

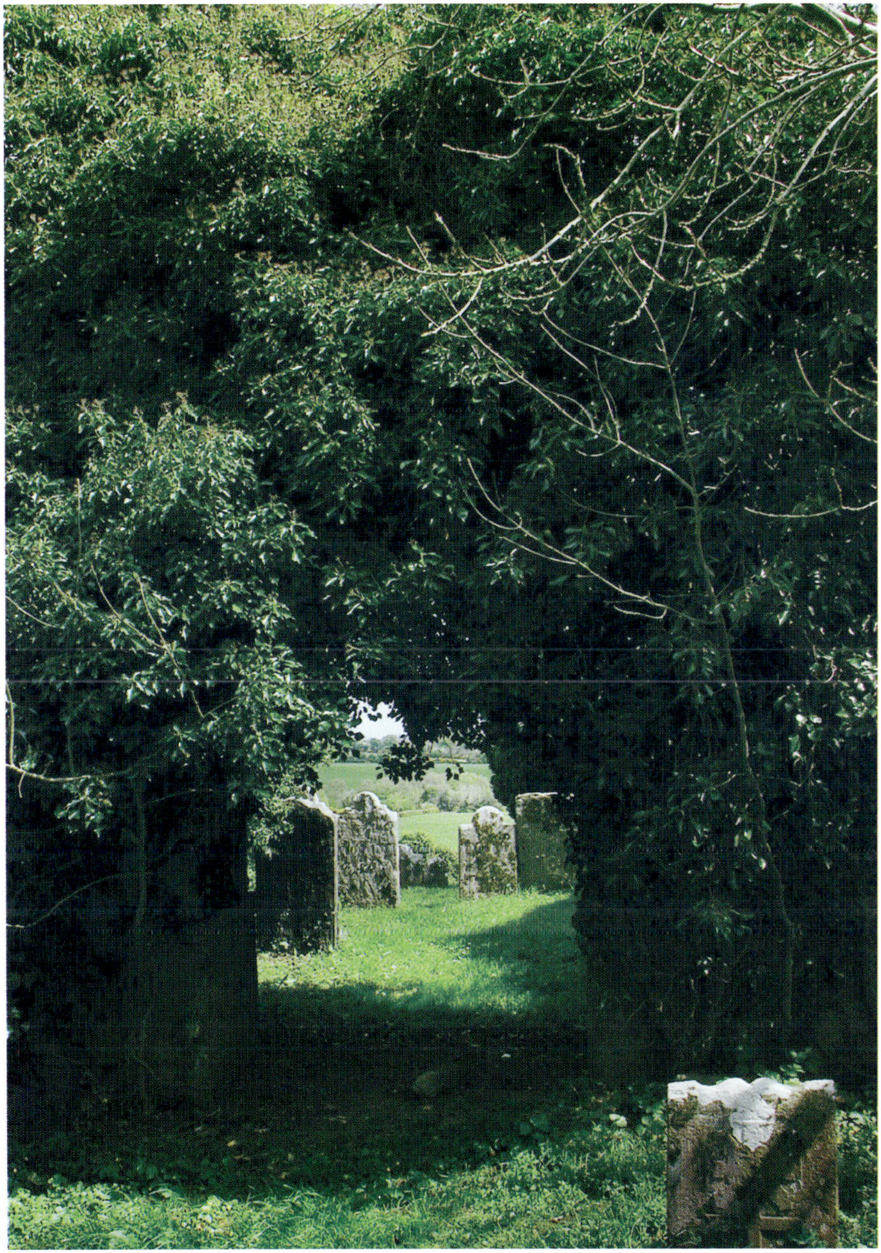

Old Graveyard, Kilrossanty

Conversation in a Country Pub

I walked in for a drink to one of the pubs in the street,
Just to pass an hour and some friends there to meet;
An old man sat in the corner drinking his pint of beer,
And to himself he was talking I couldn't help but hear.
'Twas obvious his mind wasn't with us but rambling back to the past,
Sometimes he talked very slow and at times excited and fast;
He greeted each friend as they entered into that world of his own,
If I couldn't see him but hear him I never would think him alone.

He talked of long ago matches and battles lost and won,
He talked to himself of the Tans and the time he was on the run;
Now and then he'd burst into tune and sing a verse of a song,
Then he'd continue his talking, reliving the days that are gone.
He then took out his tobacco, prepared and filled up his pipe,
I took a match from my pocket, went over and gave him a light;
His glass was getting near empty so I got up and bought him an ale,
Then I sat down and listened as he continued his tale.

"Hello Michael, how are you, and what are you drinking tonight?
Remember the time Andy was with us? We gave the Tans a great fright;
We dug a big hole in the road, and waited for the lorry to come;
The Tans jumped out of the lorry, away across the field they did run.
Is that a pint Jim you're having? I hear you're saving the hay,
I was thinking you looked a bit tired, you must be piking all day;
I hear the lads won last Sunday and that they had a great game;
What is it you're having? Sure I'll have one of the same."

"What did you think of the house dance? By God we had a great fling;
Ah those women were lively; they were the girls that could swing;
With the jigs and reels and the sets, we knocked sparks off the floor,
The sun was high in the heavens when we went out the front door.
Ah there's Johnny, he's thirsty I think; they were tarring all day;
Fill him a pint quick, he needs it; that thirst will soon go away.
I was talking to Tommie last night; he's got a job with your man down below;
He said they were cutting the corn, but 'tis lodged so the going is slow."

"I met with Mossie this morning and he was telling me this:
On his way home last night he heard music below in the Lios;
There underneath a blackthorn, by the light of a bright autumn moon,
The fairies were dancing a singing and playing a wonderful tune.
I told him he was dreaming, 'twas the drink that went to his head;
But he swore to me 'twas a fact that he never got home to his bed;
As he stood there listening and watching, he was caught in their spell,
He moved in closer and joined them and ended up dancing as well."

"Did you cut the timber, Neddy?" "Yes we cut it above on the hill."
"Will it be enough for the winter"? "Sure I hope to God that it will."
"I think we will have an old thirty, twopence a game it will do;
Ah ha Nickey, I saw you take that Joker out of your shoe!
How are the spuds with you, Paddy? The best that I've ever seen,
Sure I nearly busted today from eating spuds, mackerel and cream.
And are the mackerel plenty? No, but the boats are getting a few;
I gave three hours on the rocks and all that I caught was just two."

That old man kept on talking; he asked the question and answered himself,
Then he called for a half one, and nodded his head towards the shelf;
Again he sat back in his corner and rambled from one yarn to the next;
I drank down my pint, then wished him good luck and left.
As I made my way home I kept thinking of that sad and weary old face,
And that he was a stranger, yes a stranger in his own place;
The young people he didn't know them and I'm sure they didn't know him,
They were too involved in their own world, bright lights and a musical din.

The friend that he knew they are gone now, all his family have flown,
So he sits and drinks in his corner and makes believe that his is not alone;
In his mind he sees them again, the faces and things of his youth,
Or maybe it's all just a cover; perhaps he's afraid of the truth.
That a man could go through this world and end up alone without care,
Not a friend or relation to help him, no-one to offer a prayer;
So he sits all alone and waits, to be called to his heavenly home,
And there old friends will meet him and once more together they'll roam.

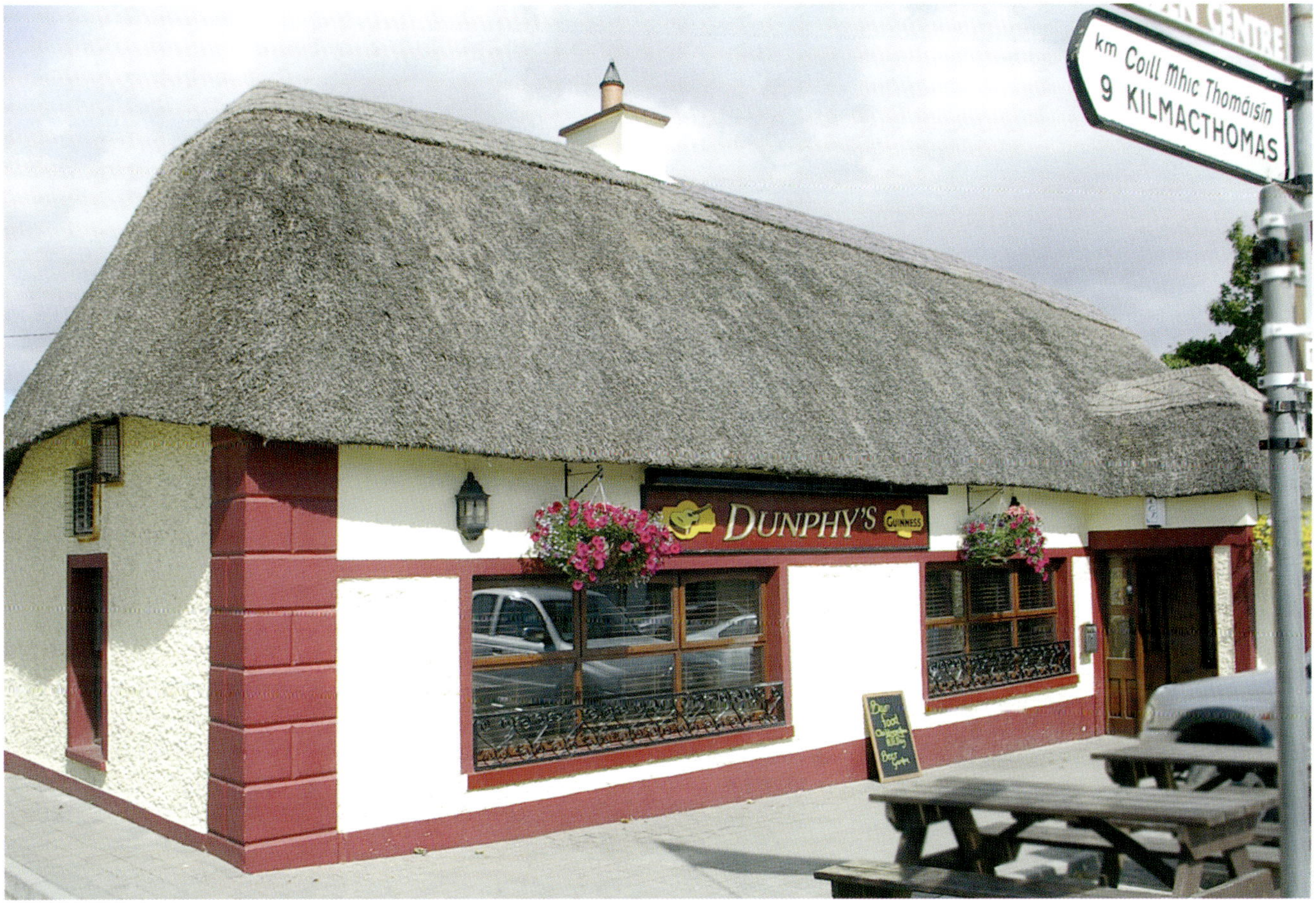

Dunphy's Pub, Kill

Copper Coast Cave

How old are you?
Are you from old God's time?
Your probably knew Methuselah's Cat as a kitten,
Have you seen many changes down through the Millennia?
Have you noticed the sounds on the road above you change?
Gone now the clip clop of the horse hooves,
Gone too the sound of the steam engines,
Replaced by cars, truck and tractors,
Are there more people swimming now than in the old days?
You must have seen thousands come here down through the years.
Do you watch the children play pirates?
I'm sure they have often hidden in your recess.
How many sand castles have you seen them build?
And then in the evening abandon them to the incoming tide,
And when the tide recedes, it is as if they never existed,
Just like many others who have stood here looking at you as I am now,
They too have vanished as if they never existed.

Do you remember the Famine?
I'm sure many people came here,
To pick dilisk, carrigeen moss and shell fish;
Anything they could eat, just to survive.
How many times have you seen Haley's Comet?
I've seen it once; I know I won't see it again.
Do you think the world is getting warmer?
They say it's global warming,
There are too many cars, planes and ships.
They've banned all the bonfires; I miss a fire in the autumn,
The smell of leaves burning, smoke wafting through the trees,
There's something homely about a bonfire, yet something primitive,
An instinct handed down to us from our ancestors,
You knew our ancestors didn't you?
Anyway I must be going now; I'm only passing through,
But compared to you, everyone and everything is just passing through,
How old are you?

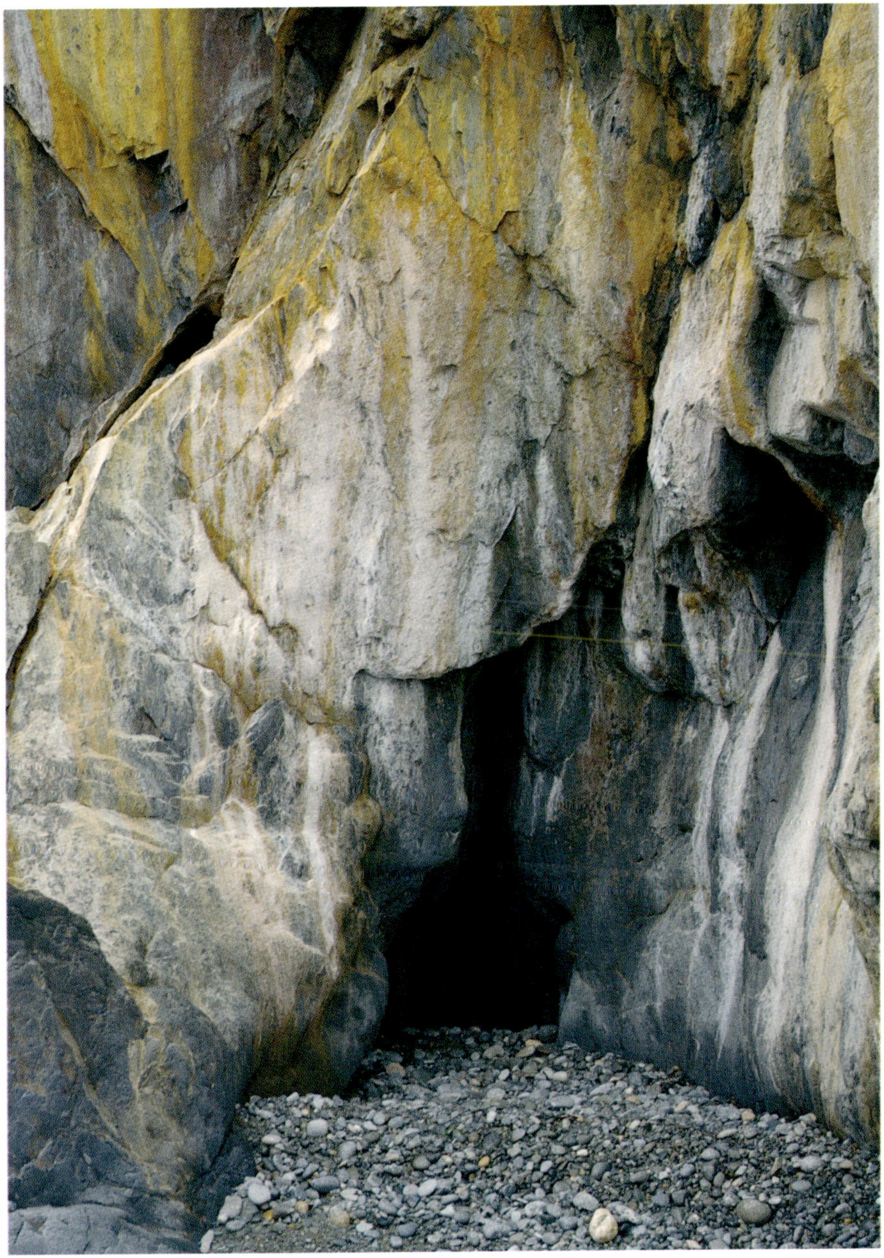

Copper Coast Cave, Ballyrooney

Dunhill Castle

Now empty and forlorn you watch the seasons come and go,
But what care you for summer sun or a fall of winter snow;
The ivy now grows green around your ancient wall,
No music now or song from within your banquet hall,
No noise around you now, but the lowing of the cattle.
But if I stand and listen I might hear the sound of battle.

Cromwell came and did lay siege – he attacked and attacked again,
But each attack was bravely met by your mistress and her men;
Around your grounds and ramparts the sound of sword and gun,
After many days of battle they had Cromwell on the run,
But then disaster struck and all because of drink,
No, not the alcoholic kind, but a keg of buttermilk.

The chief gunner was dissatisfied, he expected a stronger brew,
So above your battered walls the surrender flag he flew,
Cromwell did gain entry; revenge was in his eyes,
He then blew up the castle and the mistress bravely died;
From inside your broken walls smoke curled up to the sky,
But no one loves a traitor so Cromwell hung the gunner high.

Now a ruin you graze across the lonely Annestown bog,
Where you watched them haul the turf in summers now long gone.
You tower above the winding road a reminder of the past,
Below you now on that same road cars and tractors travel fast,
But you go back for centuries, perhaps you can recall,
When there were no roads, but just a path through oak woods big and tall.

In this peaceful valley now the song birds sweetly sing,
The River Ann flows gently by the ruined Castle of Dunhill;
And if you pass this way going to Annestown or Tramore,
As you gaze up at the Castle you might see the Mistress de le Poer;
Is that her wandering there, where she fought and died so proud,
Or perhaps it's just a trick of light, the shadow of a passing cloud.

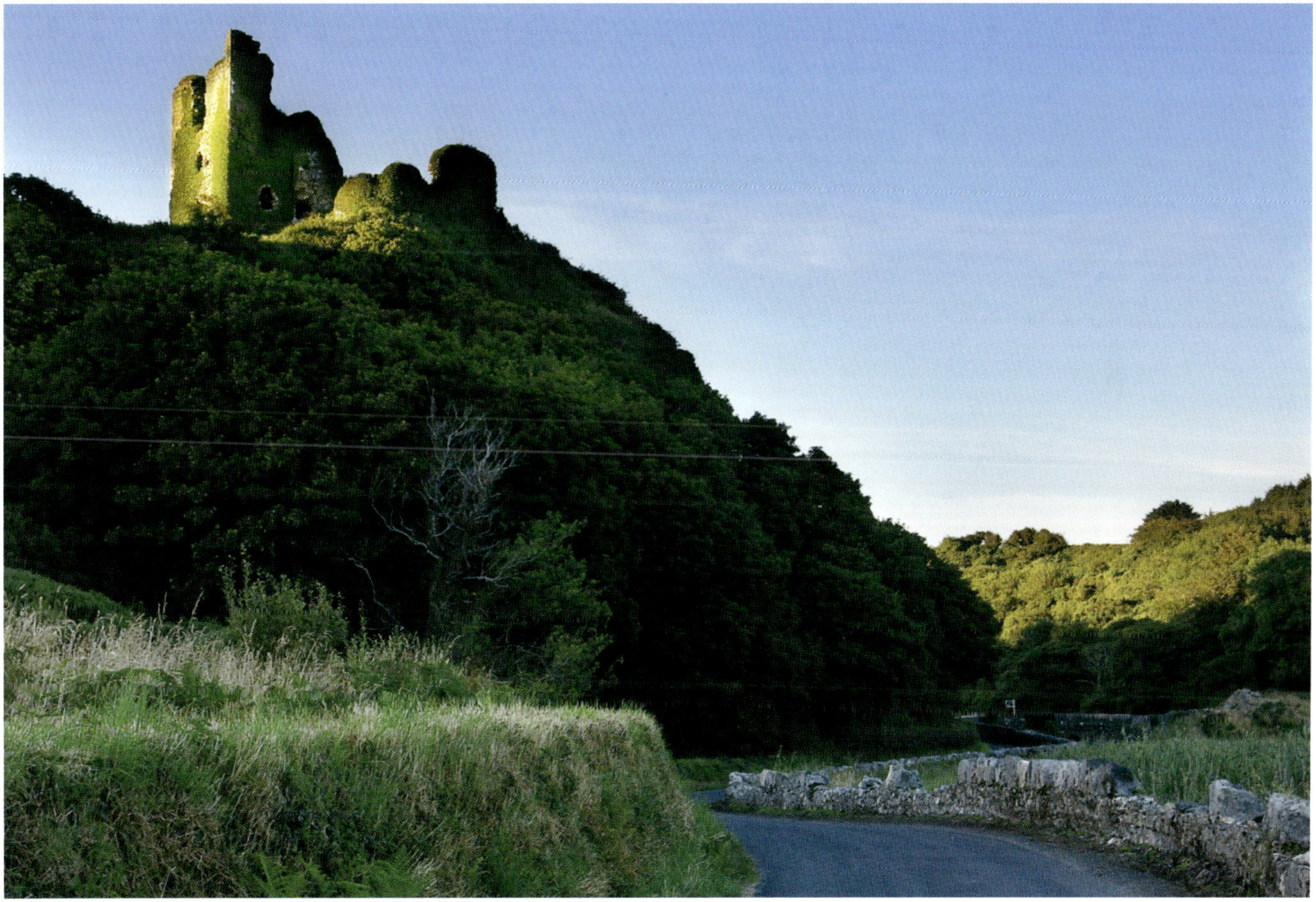

Dunhill Castle

Fields so Green

I wish I was in those fields so green
Where it's so peaceful all around,
I'd love to be in the country,
And leave this great big town.
I sit alone in this one small room,
And try and save to get back home,
But then it gets so lonely here,
I go on out and drink some beer.
Meet some friends and have a chat,
Talk of home and going back,
We wish we were in those fields so green,
Where it's peaceful all around,
We'd love to be in the country,
And leave this great big town.

But then the months roll into years,
And it breaks my heart to be still here,
I just can't seem to get away,
I drink each night what I earn each day;
But I must break drink's cursed grip,
And get away and make that trip.
It will take me back over the sea once more,
Home again to my native shore;
And once again I will be seen,
Walking through those fields of green;
And I'll hear the fox call out his cry,
Listen to birds in a summer sky,
Walk through a glen at break of day,
See a babbling brook go on its way.

Just right now I need more beer,
Maybe I'll get home next year;
But every day is getting worse,
I just can't break this awful curse.
Night and day I'm drinking more ,
I'll never see my native shore;
For scraps of food I search about,
I've become a down-and-out.
Every day I tramp these streets,
And every night on the ground I sleep;
No more I'll see those fields of green,
Where it's peaceful all around,
No more I'll see the country,
I am dying in this old town.

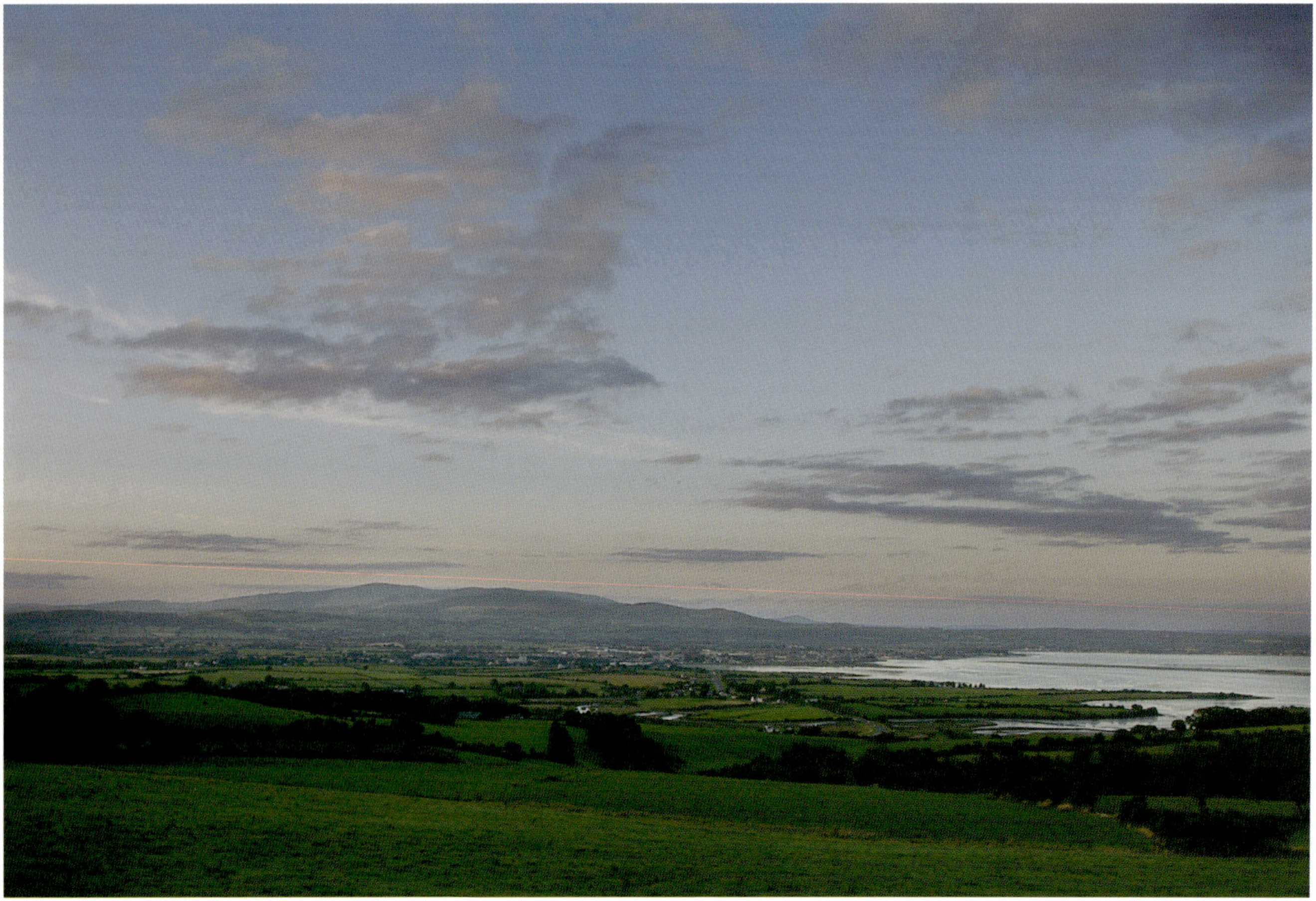

Dungarvan

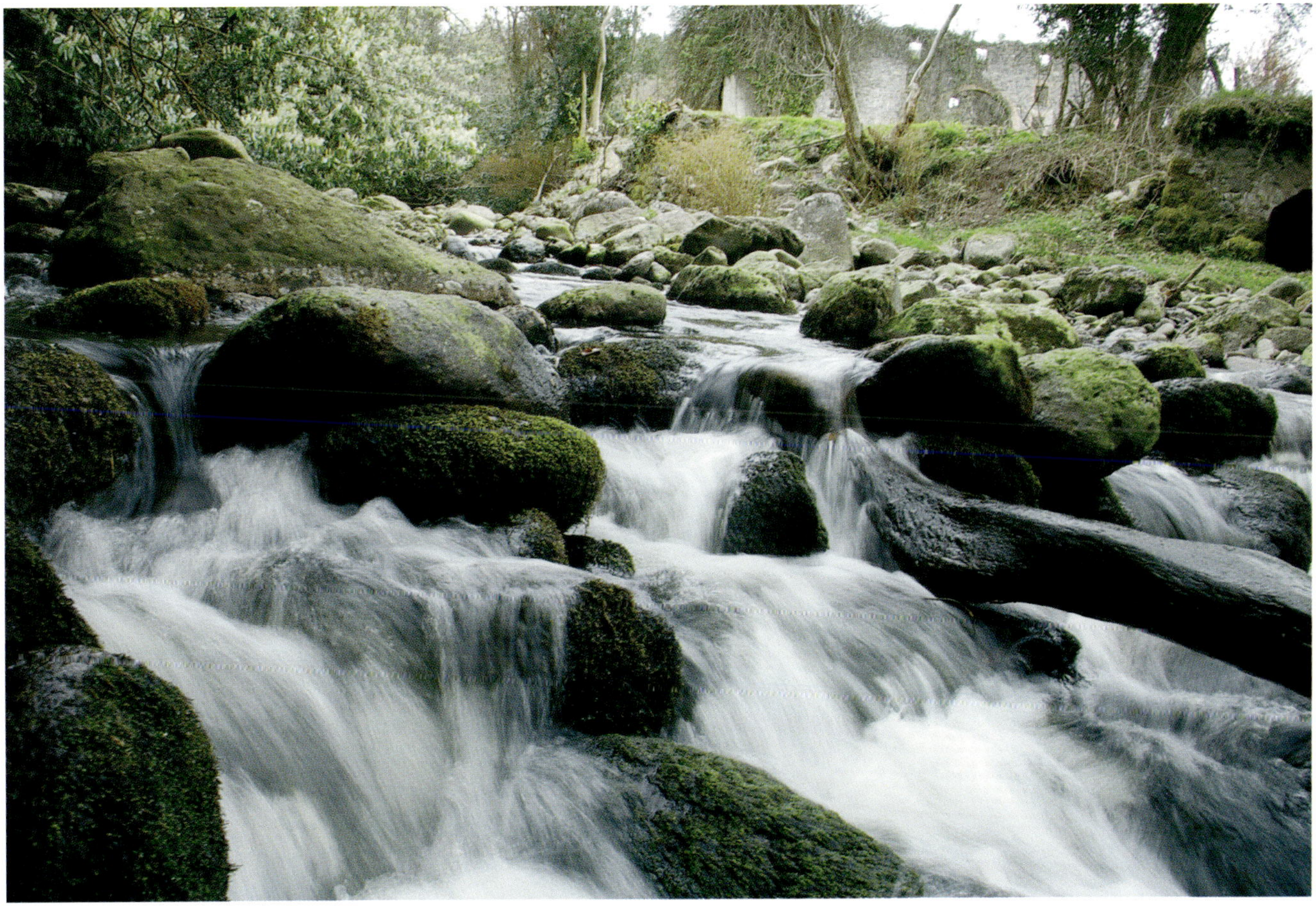

Crough Wood, Mahon Bridge

Beauty

With gasping breath and unbelieving eye,
I gazed on a beautiful vale under a clear blue sky,
Was I dreaming, was I awake?
Such beauty my heart would not take,
But there it was before me laid;
The beauty of the world, in a peaceful glade.
Beauty, fire of the heart, with peace cover the earth,
Beauty to know you live, is more joyful,
Than a winter's day giving way to spring.
Beauty, you are there, so wonderful, so brave,
Like an elegant yacht on a crested wave,
A precious gem for all to see,
Created by nature for you and me.
I turn my head I look around,
Look at the sky and at the ground,
And everywhere I can see,
What a wonderful place this world can be.

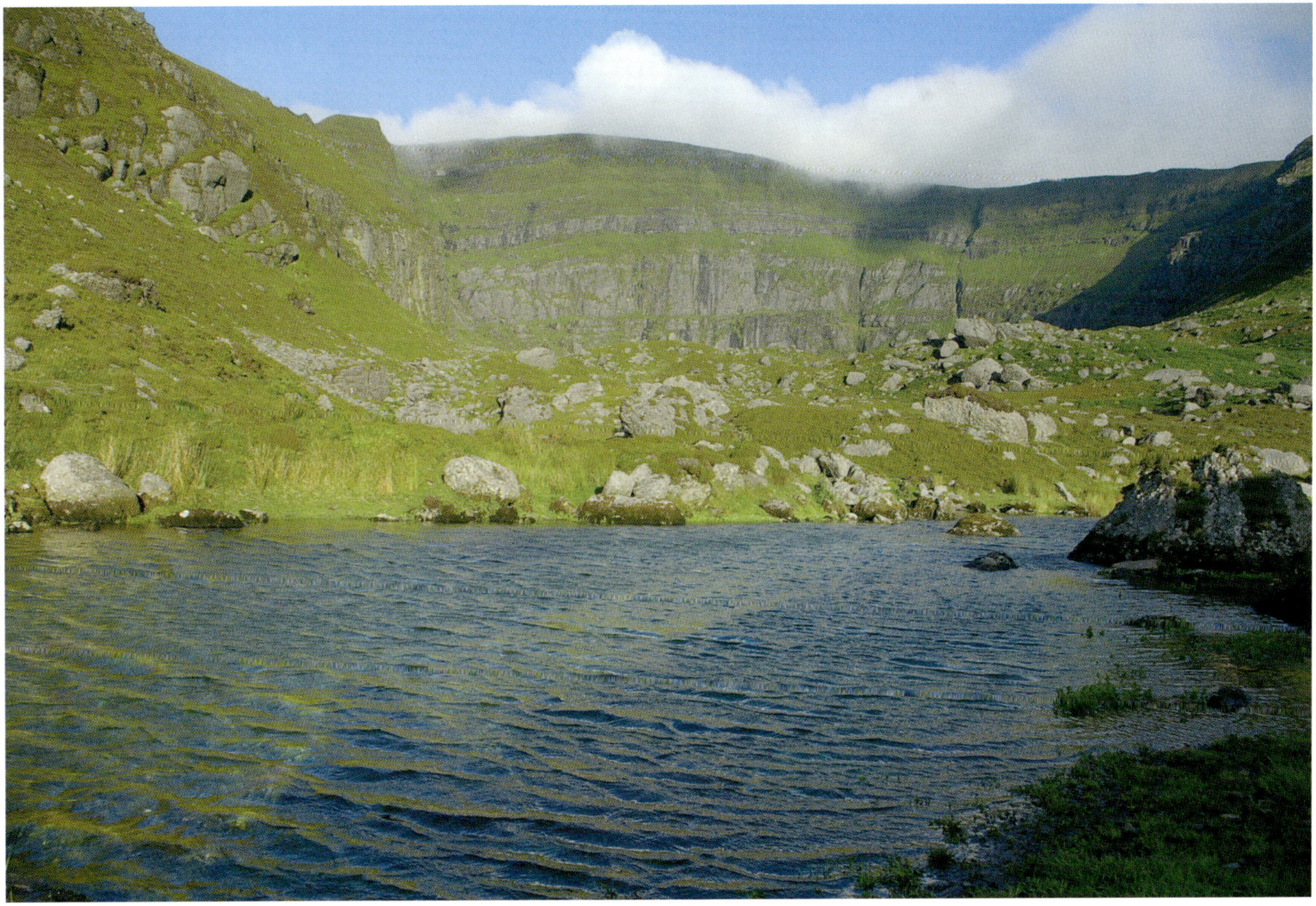

Coumshingaun, Comeragh Mountains

Life and Seasons

Spring, when sap stirs in the trees and all things begin to grow,
Warm sun creeps in hidden corners and melts the last of winter's snow;
Now the ever increasing chatter of birds tell us once more its springtime,
Hibernating animals awake from sleep and emerge into warm sunshine,
They gaze in wonder upon the world, like a baby's first view of life;
A life that lies tantalizing ahead with all things good and no thoughts of strife,
Spring the baby of the seasons, when every day brings something new,
Blossoms bloom and trees grow green and the baby is growing too.

Summer and all its energetic activities running, playing, swimming, so many happy hours.
Then first love and kiss and the world sparkles like sunshine after summer showers;
Long summer days drift into short summer nights and two hearts beat as one,
Birds in an all day search for food to feed their every hungry young.
Season of colourful flowers and happy hearts, dancing, singing and seaside play
Birds and bees and other summer sounds form a choir to sing you through the day,
Summer, the teenage season, when the world is perfect and there are so many things to do.
The cornfields turn to gold, the cuckoo's going and summer is going too.

Autumn coloured golden brown, ripened fruit is picked for store,
The swallows in lines along the wires are preparing to fly away once more,
Autumn evenings, the scent of bonfire smoke and we go walking, kicking leaves,
The squirrels are busy gathering nuts, as they run from tree to tree.
The corn is cut and saved, days grow short and nights grow longer,
Our summer love has borne its fruit and every day they grow big and stronger;
Autumn, season of middle age, when hair turns grey and life slows down,
Then a cold gust of wind and the last clinging leaves fall to ground.

Winter comes, the world takes on an empty look, fields are bare and still,
We sit by the fire; our world now consists of a window view of a nearby hill,
The first frost and snow, days of pension books and pills, all is damp and cold,
Days now spent from bed to fire, limbs now aching tired and old.
Dark cold winter days spent in loneliness and memories of the past,
Now the final realisation that life is just a passing phase, nothing is made to last,
Winter season of old age waiting for the day, when this world and I will part,
And when God calls, hopefully in heaven, another spring will start.

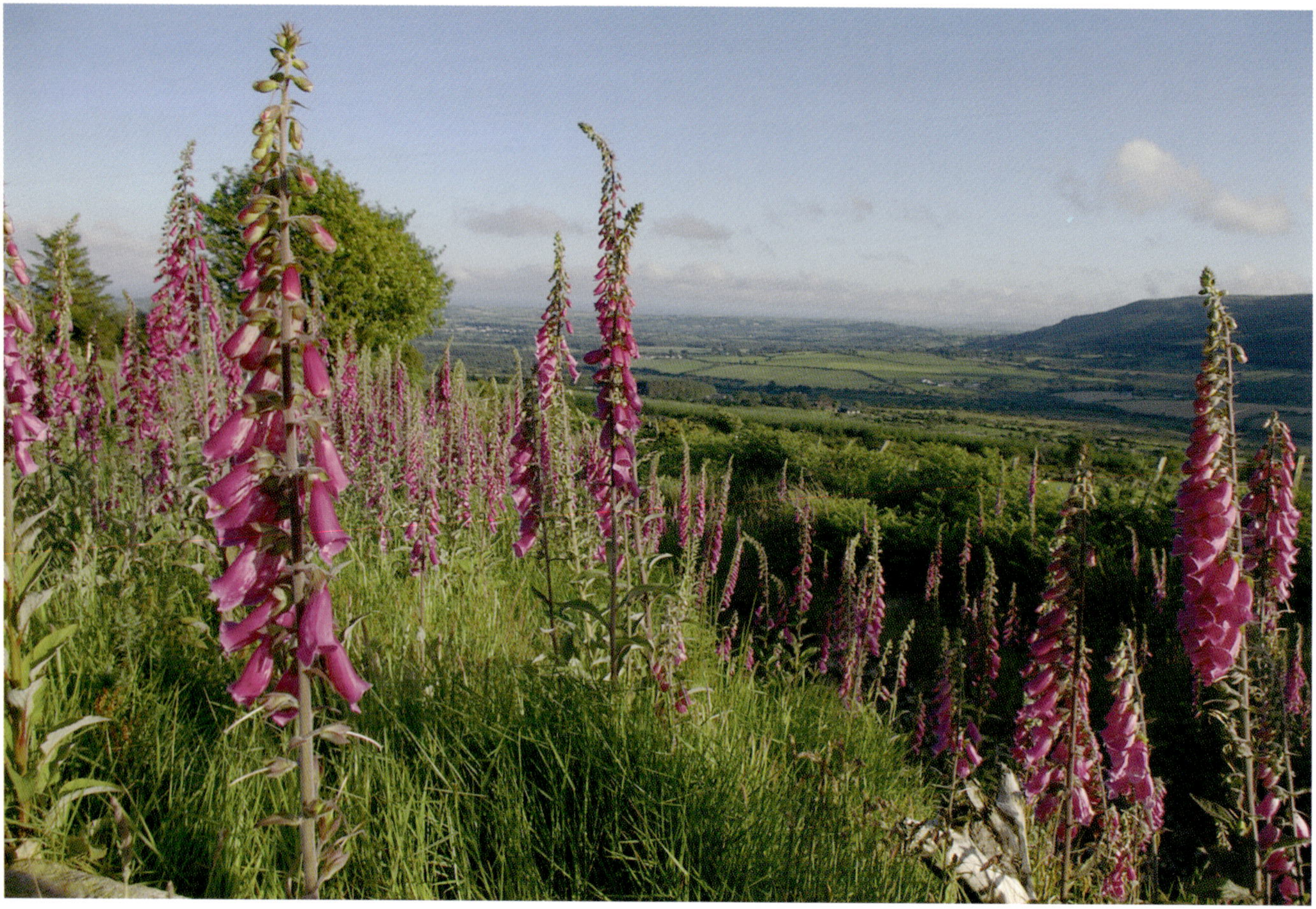

'Foxglove Field', Comeragh

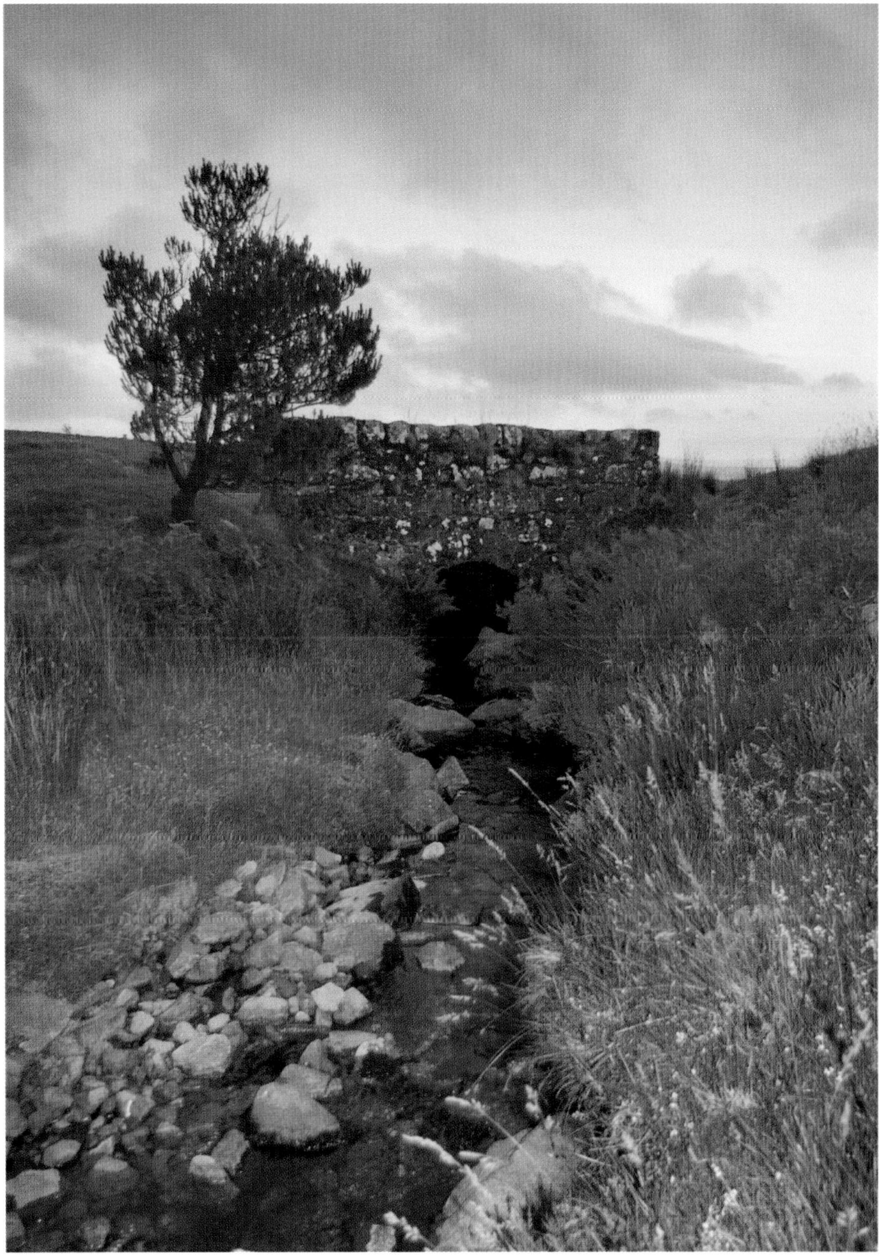

Mauma Road, Kilbrien

Half An Autumn's Morn'

I stood and watched the combine move through that field of corn,
It cut and threshed that field of oats in half an autumn's morn';
I watched the tractor move in close, the ripened grain to take,
I listened, but alas in vain, to hear the corncrake.
To my mind then came a vision of that field of long ago,
And all the work that it would take, that field of oats to grow.
Two horses, man, and one sod plough turned that field from green to brown,
"Go on, keep off, come in!" words you'd hear, as seagulls circled round;
And then would come the harrow, that would keep you fit,
As all day long you walked behind, as the horses chomped the bit;
Manure and then the sower and half the work was done,
Then you prayed for the April showers, followed by the summer sun.

Coming across the valley, carried on a gentle breeze,
The sound of the reaper and binder circling the field;
As the standing corn got smaller, of the bundles there were more,
They were gathered by the workmen into stooks of four;
From stooks they would make stacks, that was a special skill,
As a youth I learned to make them, I could make them still.
Once more they'd tackle horses, this time to haul a cart,
They'd haul the corn to the haggard and on the rick they'd start;
And when they had it finished, sure they'd feel very proud,
You would see them walk around it, and survey it from the ground;
Soon would come the thresher and give two days threshing corn,
But now they cut and thresh in half an autumn's morn'.

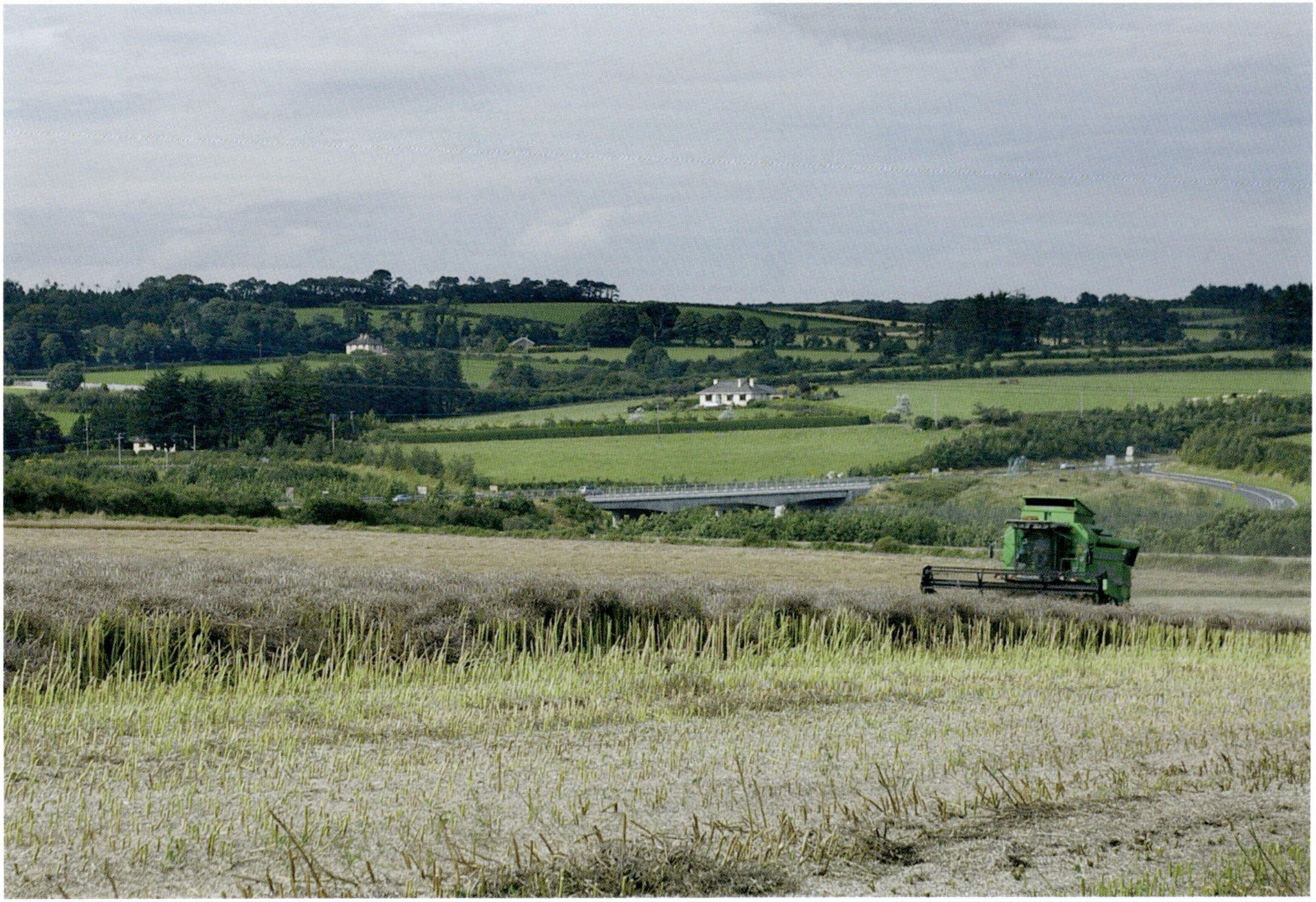

Combine Harvester, Kilmacthomas

The Magic Road

Is it an optical illusion?
Or am I suffering from delusion?
I'm feeling quite perplexed,
A certain problem has me vexed;
That's the law of gravity,
And how it applies to you and me.

It can never be denied,
No matter how and when you tried,
Why did my car go up the hill?
Up and up of it's own free will.
Now you may not think that's stunning,
But the engine was not running.

The Comeraghs are a lovely place,
Beautiful scenery and open space,
If and when you wander there,
I warn you now take great care,
And listen to what the locals say;
Supernatural forces are at play.

When you're on the Magic Road,
By yourself or with a load,
You park your car on that decline,
I'll tell you now what happened mine;
With handbrake off and engine cut,
It started climbing up and up.

Moving swiftly up that slope,
And not a sign of towing rope,
It was near the Mahon Falls,
No-one around that I could call,
On and on up over the brow,
You won't believe what happened now:

In the distance I heard a crash,
Followed by a mighty splash,
I asked myself how this could happen,
Then I heard the sound of laughin',
I turned around and there and then,
I saw movement in the glen.

I went down to search around,
To try and find this laughing sound,
I tripped up and fell in the river,
Now I sit on the bank and shiver.
One thing now I want to know,
How up that hill my car could go?

So have you got an explanation?
I put this question to the nation;
Is it an optical illusion?
Or am I suffering from delusion?
Or is it what the locals say,
Supernatural forces are at play.

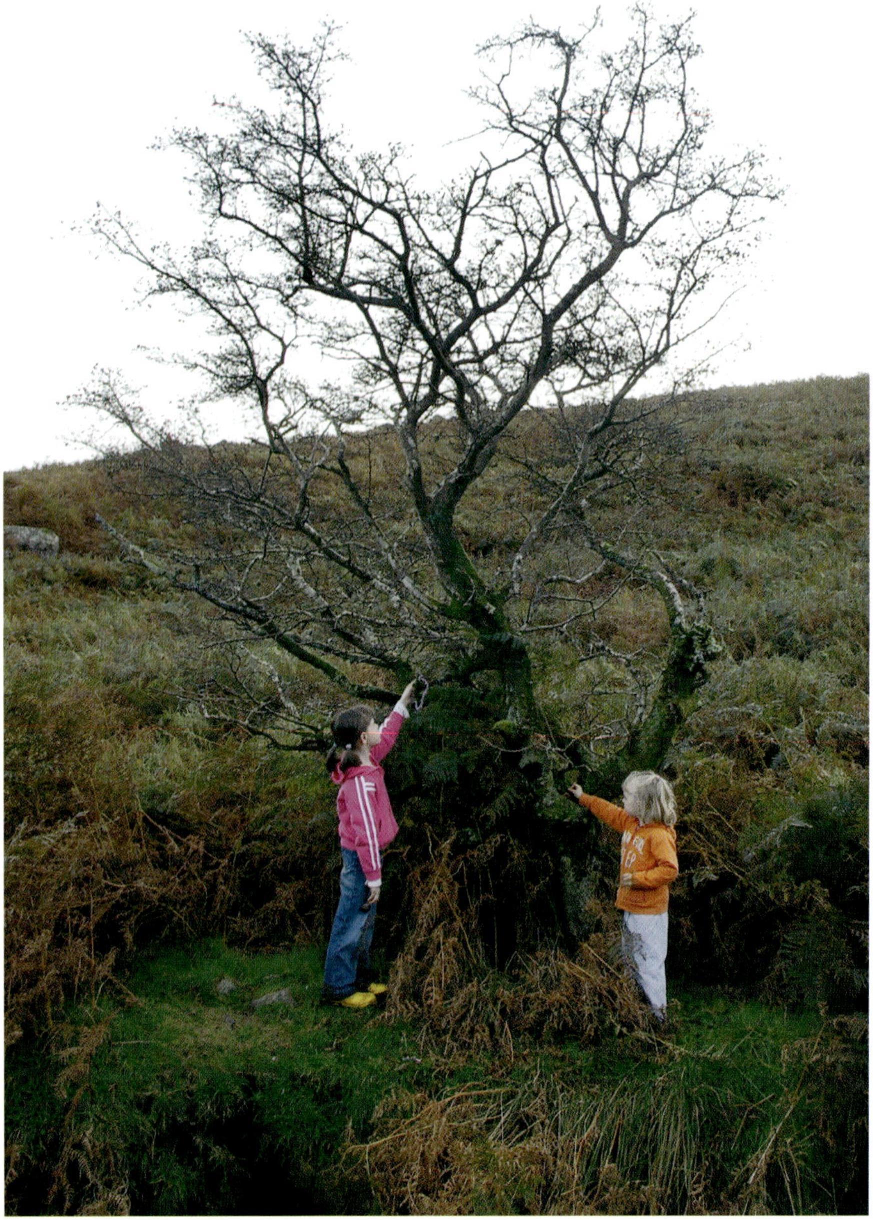

'Pixie Bush', Comeragh Mountains

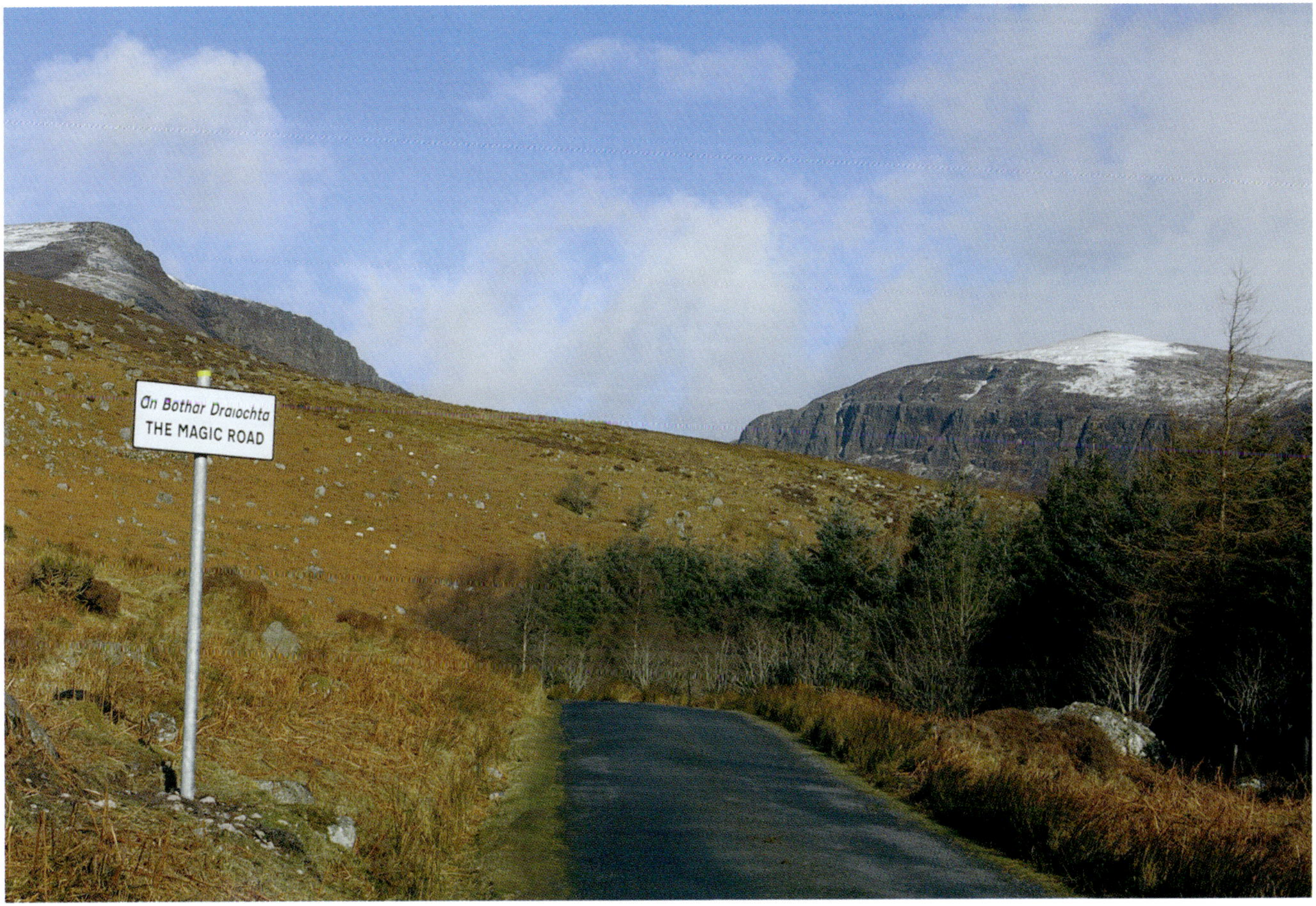

The Magic Road, Comeragh Mountains

Peace and Love

Summer evening, under skies of blue,
I'll stroll through shady lanes with you,
We'll live in a dreamlike world,
Of happiness and Christmas bells,
We'll watch our love unfurl,
As we stroll through glistening dells,
When winter days turn to spring,
And evening ever growing longer,
We'll sit and listen to all birds sing,
And know are love is growing stronger,
On our world, this war-torn earth,
Men are striving to annihilate each other,
But we'll find contentment by a glowing hearth,
And never lift a hand to kill a brother.
We'll build our home on the clouds above,
Far far away from man's self made grief,
Live to our own ideals of love,
And not be dictated to by other mans beliefs.
This world is heading for total ruin,
No more beauty for the eye to see,
But they can't blame us love, for what they're doing.
Hold my hand love; we'll just live love for you and me.

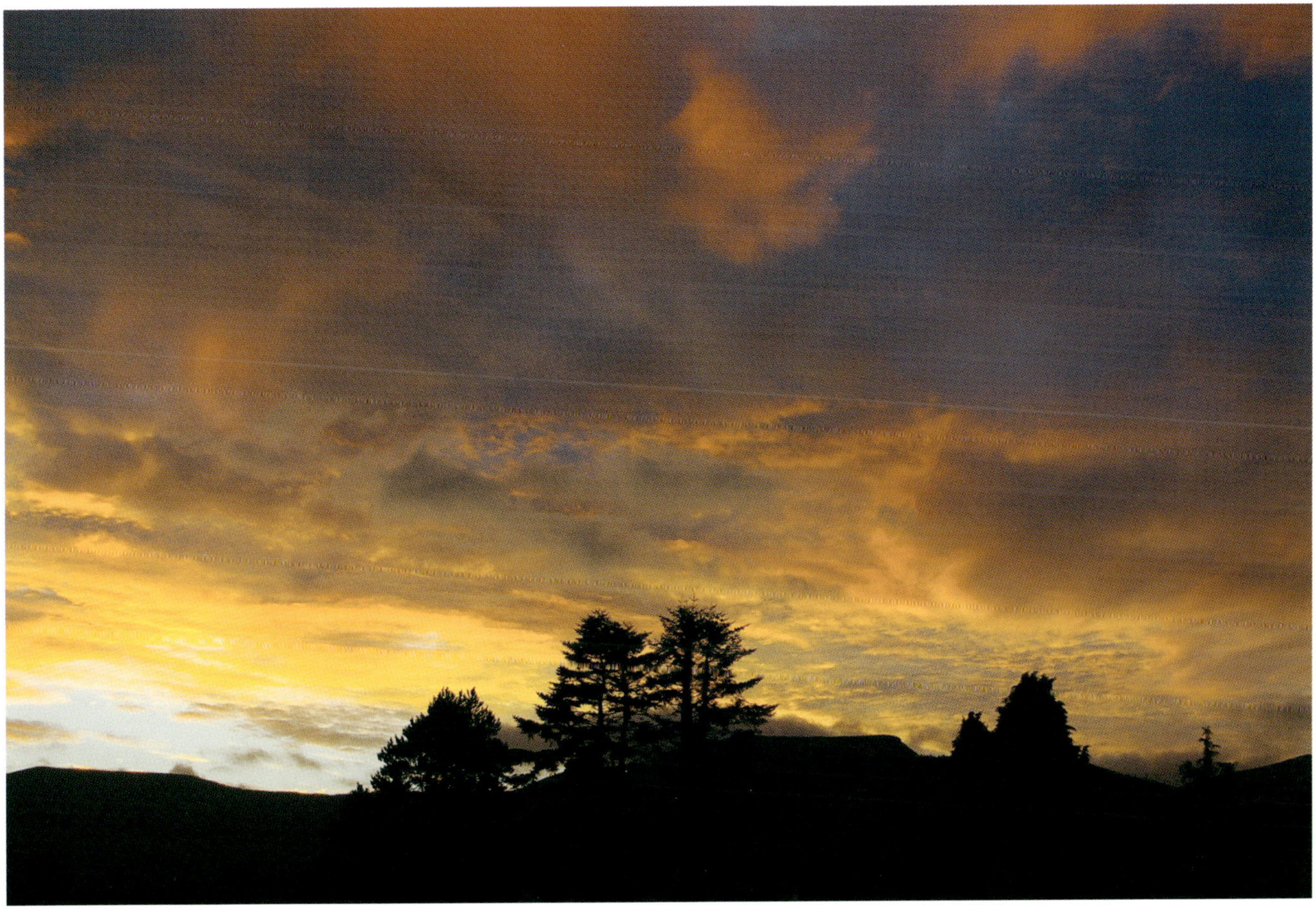

'Fire', Comeragh Mountains

My Déise Love

Oh Déise my home, the fairest of all,
Though now far away, I still hear you call,
If I had the chance to go back through the years
I'd stay in the Déise, with the one I love dear.
She was everything to me, I loved her so,
But from her and the Déise, I had to go,
Around this old world I was destined to roam,
Far away from my love and my own Déise home.

My love in the Déise is so dear to me,
Her smile is as bright as the sun on the sea,
Her eyes are as clear as a sparkling lake,
Oh my sweet love many hearts you will break.
My love and my Déise, my pride and delight,
I'm so proud of you and the blue and the white,
To you, my own love, none can compare,
Just like the Déise, a jewel so rare.

I've travelled the Déise, from east to the west,
Through lovely green valley to high mountain crest,
From the wilds of the Comeraghs to the blue of the sea,
Oh lovely Déise, you're heaven to me.
My love's in the Déise, the place I call home,
By the banks of your rivers I long to roam,
The Suir and the Blackwater are so dear to me,
Again watch the Mahon flow down to the sea.

Your valleys and mountains to ramble once more,
To walk once again along your seashore,
The faces and places I saw as a boy,
I think of them now with a tear in my eye.
My love and my Déise, I'll praise you out loud,
Because of you both I'm ever so proud,
There are many fair gems on this island, that's true,
But none can compare with the Déise and you.

I miss the Déise, my love I miss too,
I must return to my Déise and you,
I hope you are waiting, I love you so,
My love and my Déise, to you I must go.
When soft breezes blow in from the ocean so wide,
I'll stroll through green valleys with you by my side,
When the birds in the summer sing their sweet song,
With my love in the Déise, that's where I belong.

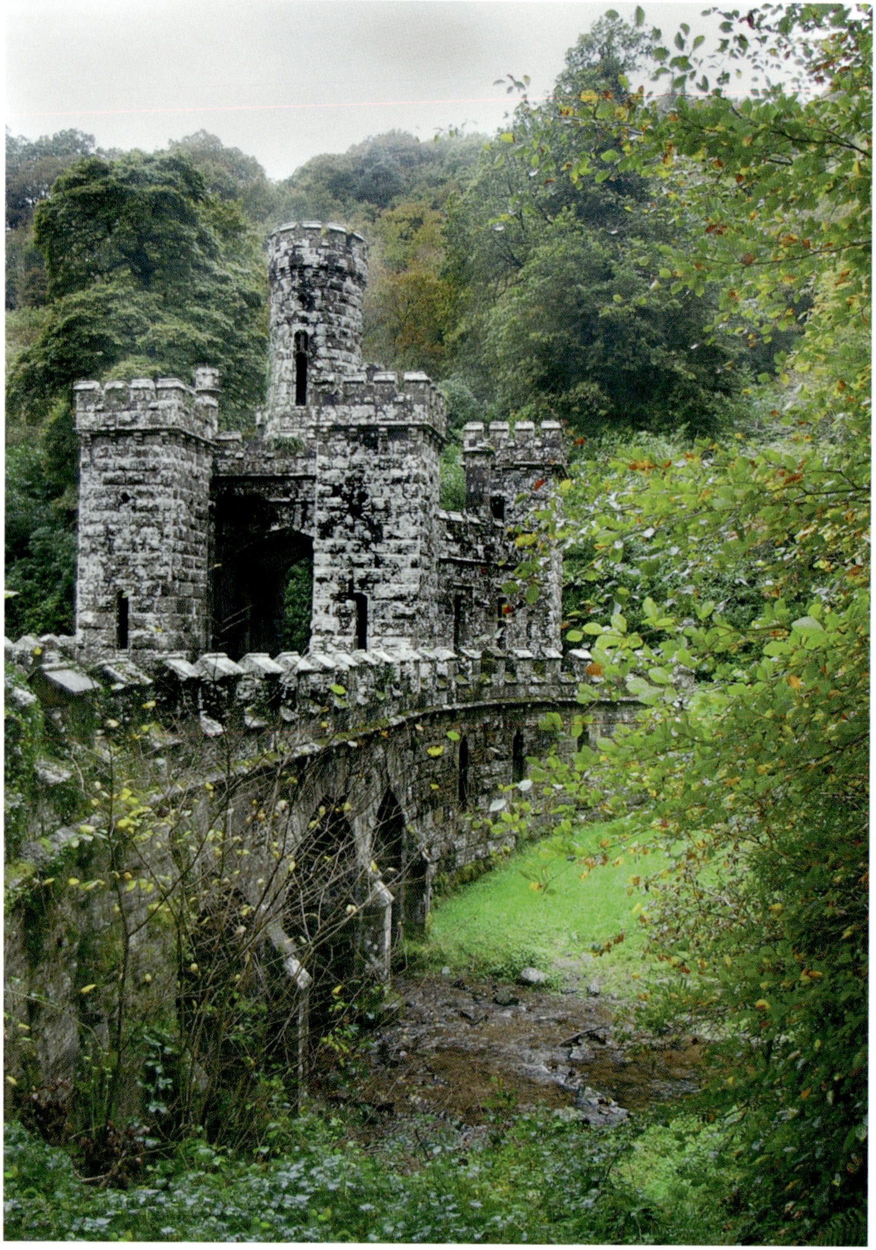

The Towers, Lismore

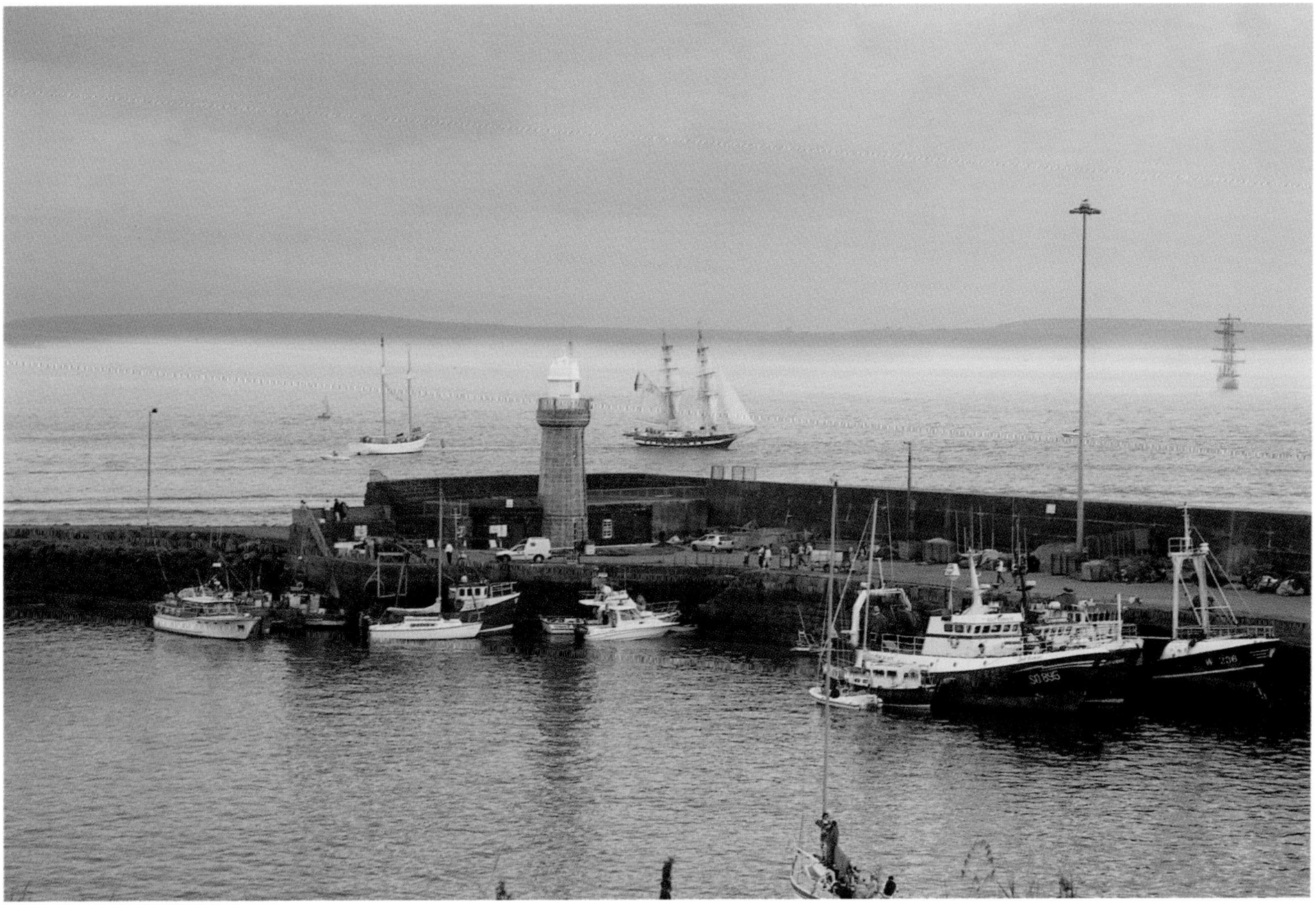

Dunmore East

Steam Engine

She moved towards the village in a cloud of smoke and steam,
My children could not believe it, what is this strange machine?
They stood and gazed in wonder, a sight they never saw before,
This lovely old steam engine going slowly past our door;
And with it came fond memories to those of us that are older,
As I stood and watched with my young child on my shoulder.

This lovely old steam engine, a survivor from the past,
She had her days of glory when this world didn't go so fast;
In the days before the combine and the modern silorater,
She would go from farm to farm with thresher and elevator.
She would travel through the country, steam over hill and vale,
She shared the roads of Ireland with the donkey and Clydesdale.

A tell-tale plume of smoke, a yell and she's on her way,
That farmyard would buzz on those far-off threshing days;
They would shovel in the coal and really build up steam,
And all would work as one, man, thresher and machine.
From dawn till dusk they gave their all,
As one rick got large, the other small.

The children laughed and played about,
And thirsts were quenched with pints of stout,
They would bank her down for the hours of night,
And off again at dawn's first light;
Stoke her up and be on her way,
Another threshing, another day.

The smell of burning coal is in the air,
That old machine stands graceful there,
With the help of skilful hands she will survive,
To serve as a bridge across the gap of time;
Brought from the past to be with us here,
For all of us, a chance to view yesteryear.

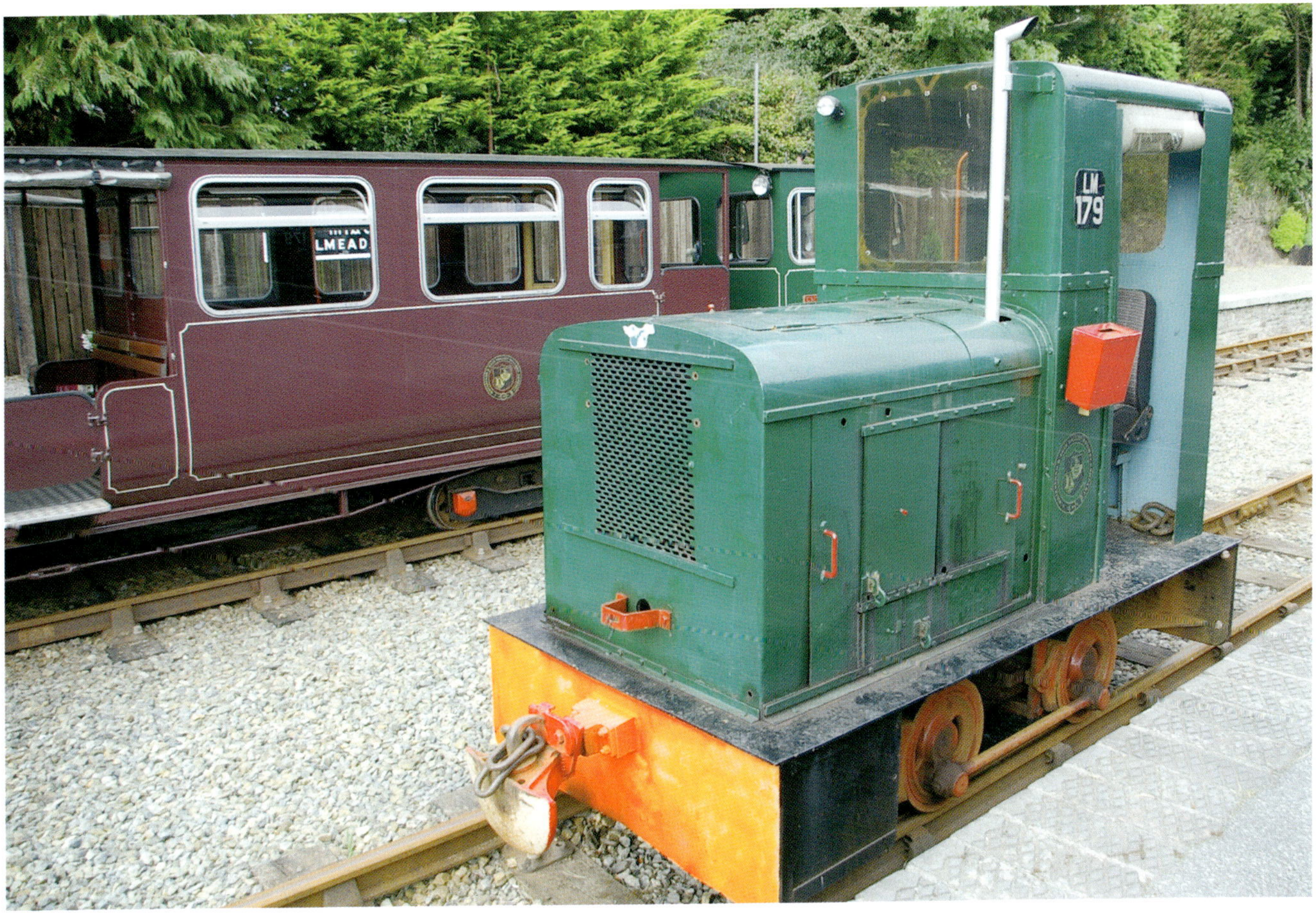

Kilmeaden Railway

Returning

Down the road he walked and there just around the bend,
Stood an ivy covered ruin that was his journey's end.
Some thousand miles he traveled for something seemed to call,
The voices of his ancestors, born inside those homely walls.
As he stands outside that place now empty and decayed,
He looks around at quiet fields,
Where his forebearers worked and played.
From down to fall of night, so hard they had to toil,
For their food upon the table, they depended on the soil.
Then came a year, when the potato crop did fail,
From valley and from mountain, came an agonizing wail.

The spectre of starvation cast its shadow across the land,
Thousands died from hunger, while others lived so grand,
Evicted and burnt out, cast on the side of the road,
Families torn asunder, dying in the wet and cold,
Ragged covered walking bones, not dead yet not alive,
Scavenging the country, desperate to survive.
Ireland turned to America, in those grief filled years,
You threw her out a lifeboat, when she was swamped in tears;
Our hard working sons and daughters found refuge on your shore,
You gave to them a welcome; you never closed your door.

They sailed across the Atlantic, from hunger and from strife,
In our darkest hour, you were a guiding light,
A real good friend and neighbour, you helped them through the pain,
You gave a home and work, restored their pride again.
And they returned their gratitude in sweat, tears and blood,
They helped to build your railroad, across mountain, plain and flood.
They joined your armed forces, fought for the stars and stripes,
And when you lost John Kennedy, they cried with you that night.
You took in our emigrants, they proved loyal and true,
You gave to them a home, and they gave back to you.

Distinguished sons and daughters, who worked with heart and hand,
Descendants of those emigrants became presidents of your land;
And now some are returning, to their forebearers' native soil,
But not in rags and poverty, they return in style.
And a land that once was barren, is now bountiful again,
But the Famine is not forgotten here, or the poverty and pain,
As you walk among us, and trod your forebearers sod,
We will all remember those who starved in field and bog,
America we will remember it was you who gave the call,
And said "come on, I'll help you, there's plenty here for all".

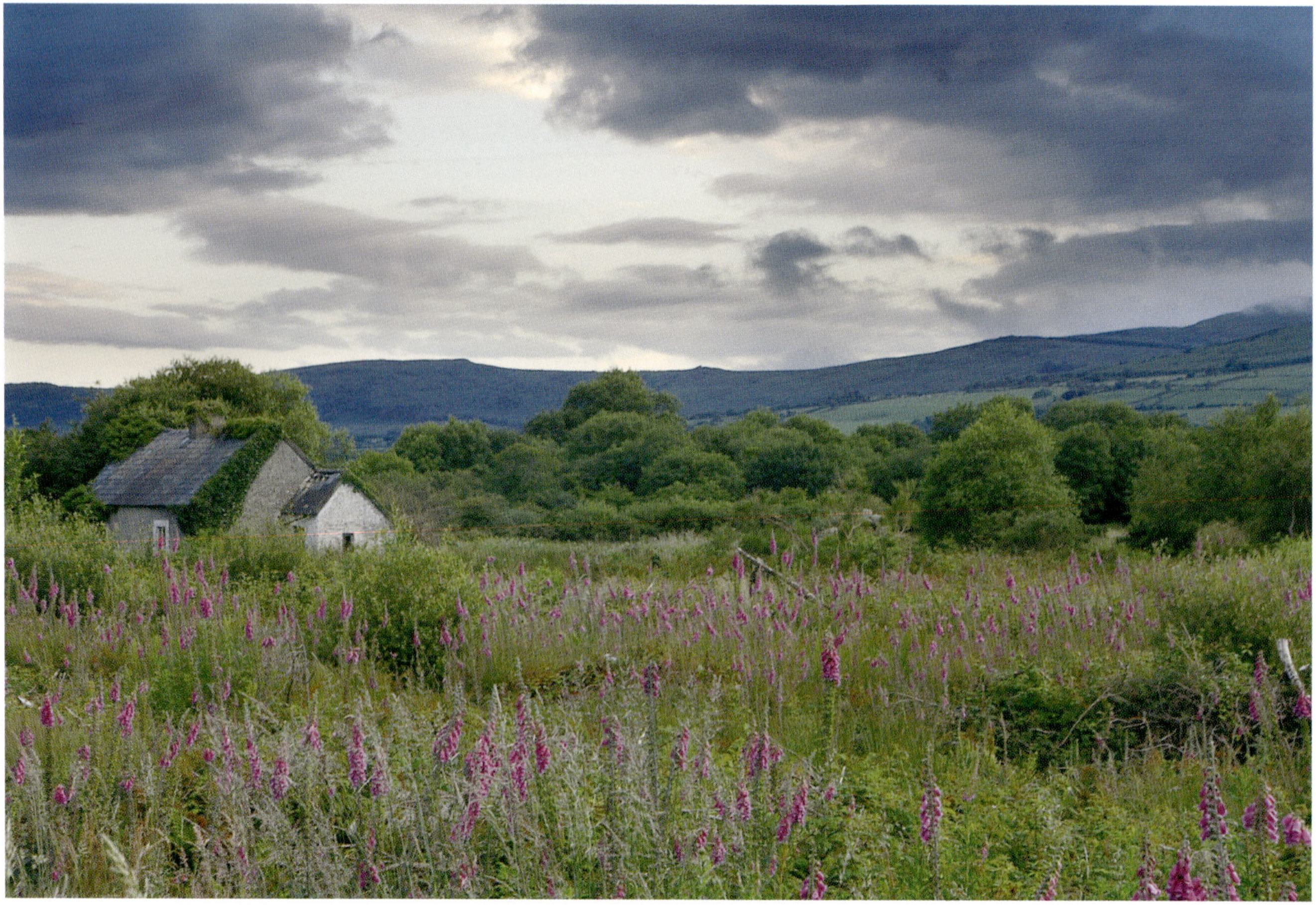

Old Cottage, Lemybrien

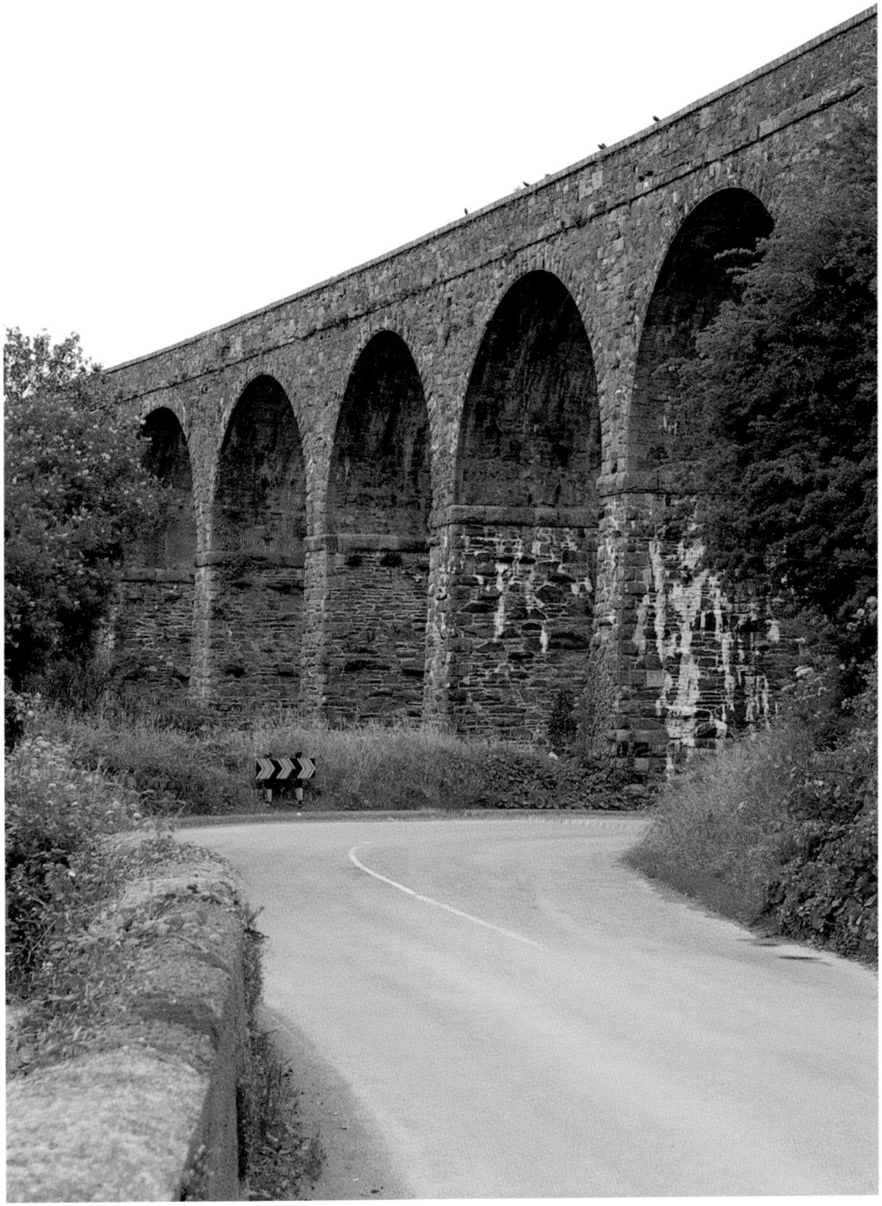

Mahon Railway Viaduct, Kilmacthomas

The Long Long Road to Croker

On the long long road to Croker, there's joy if you reach the end,
But there are many hills to climb and several dangerous bends;
For the long long road to Croker has shattered many teams,
There are tears in every pothole and the lines are broken dreams.
Another year is over; it ends once more in pain,
But the Déise's quest for glory shall not be in vain;
We have the men, they have the skill, of that I have no doubt,
And to conquer the road to Croker, once more they must set out.

In pursuit of Liam McCarthy, that famed elusive cup,
Its at the end of the road to Croker, our boys will not give up;
The Rebels will lay in ambush, and try to end our dream,
The Cats they will be waiting, hoping to take the cream.
Limerick will be no lady and the Premier County, Tipp.
Will have a plan and try to sink the famed three Déise ships,
And the boys from the Slaney, the Banner men from Clare,
Will try their best, so will all the rest, to stop us getting there.

On the long long road to Croker, you must beat all the rest,
And come All-Ireland Sunday, bravely stand up to the test;
But don't be too downhearted, you must keep the faith,
You are the men to fulfil the dream and end those years of wait;
So in winter, well have your rest, you deserve it that is true,
Then back on the road to Croker, proudly wearing the white and blue.
So live in hope, keep the dream, soon will come your time,
Then we'll wrap you all in glory, like the men of fifty nine.

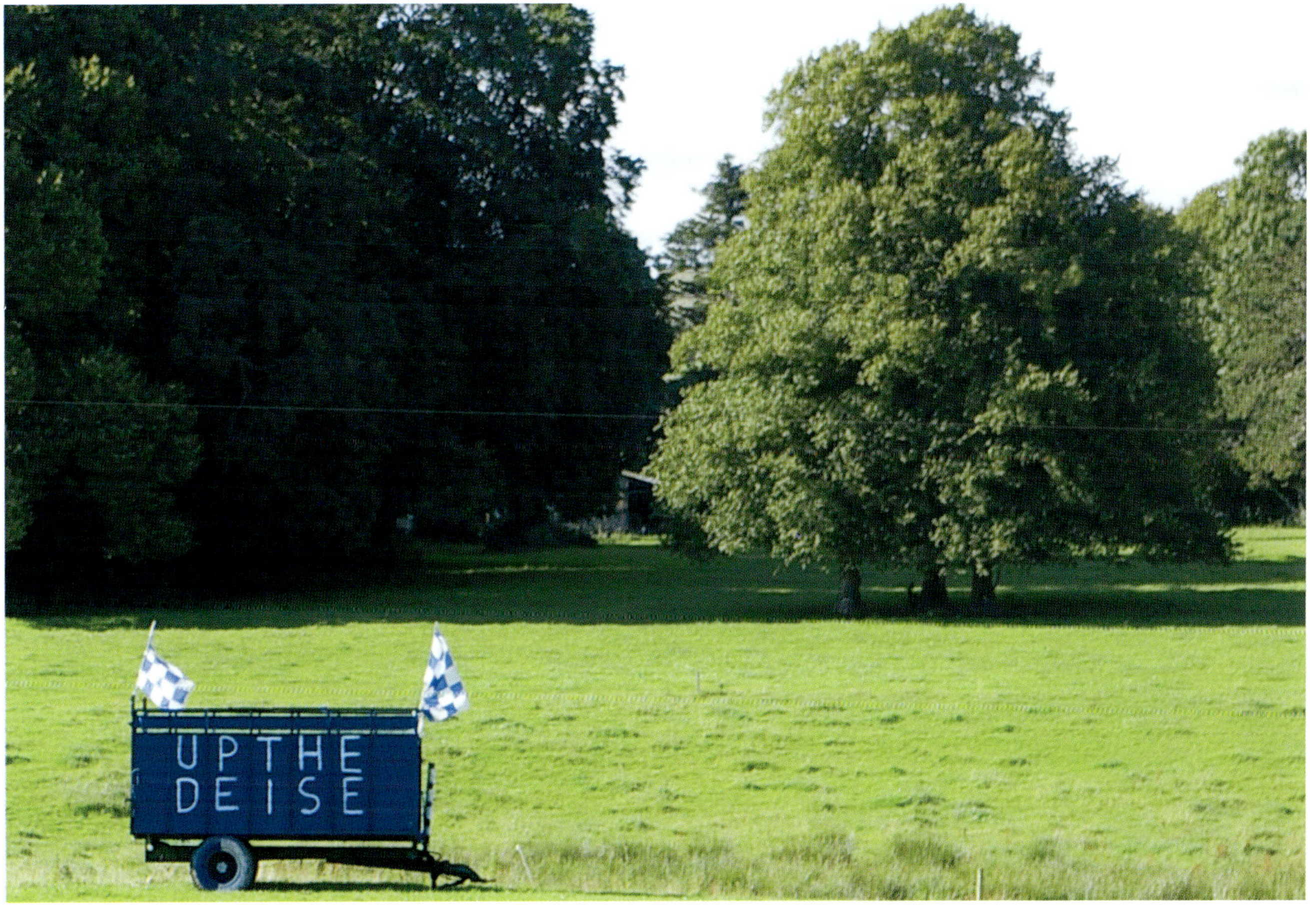

'Up the Déise' Trailer, Kilmeaden

Rambling Pat

He was sheltered from the North-east wind by a high furze covered ditch,
His donkey was tied to a blackthorn sceach and also his mongrel bitch,
The donkey's car was coloured green; the wheels were black and red,
Beside the car a tattered tent and inside a dry straw bed.
An old black kettle was on the fire, the flames danced in the breeze,
A blackbird sang in a nearby bush, the smoke curled through the trees,
He sat upon a rotten log and asked me the time of day,
He offered me his hand-made mug, said "would you like some tay?"
I moved a stone close to the fire and sat down for a chat,
He said his trade was travelling and to call him Rambling Pat.

The two of us sat round the fire in the grey frost covered vale,
He lit his pipe, I sipped some tea and he began his tale;
"I started life seventy years ago on a sun-drenched summer morn',
To the sound of birds on the side of the road, that's where I was born,
I opened my mouth and breathed in God's fresh, free given air,
My mother wrapped me in her coloured shawl; I travelled on from there;
I rambled round high mountains and travelled valleys green,
The beauty of this country, all of it I've seen,
I've knocked on doors, asked for food, offered to pay in kind,
'Tis many the stone of spuds I've picked and many a saddle shined.

"I've helped out at the threshing and cocked some fields of hay,
I've danced 'til dawn then packed my things again be on my way,
Down the road around the bend some new place to view,
An ass to buy, a pony sell, or clean a chimney flue.
Sometimes I'd go from house to house mending pots and pans,
And at the Fairs I'd sell my mugs and fine one-gallon cans.
I've slept outside on summer nights, the stars shining overhead,
I've sheltered from the rain and snow, in some friendly farmer's shed.
I'd spin a tale to boys and girls sitting on their mother's knee,
The labourer and his family always welcomed me."

He poked the fire, threw in a stick, tapped his pipe on the log,
And said "soon I'll have to leave valley, mountain and bog;
Failing health, I am getting old; they say I shouldn't be alone,
But I'll do whatever I can to avoid an old people's home."
I emptied my mug, said my thanks for the tea, hope to see you again,
I drove away and waved my hand to one of the travelling men,
A year has passed since I dined with him; I wonder is he rambling still,
And is his smoke curling up from the foot of an Irish hill?
Or perhaps on some cold frosty morn' he failed to hear the fox's cry,
And now his soul is rambling free through the heavenly roads in the sky.

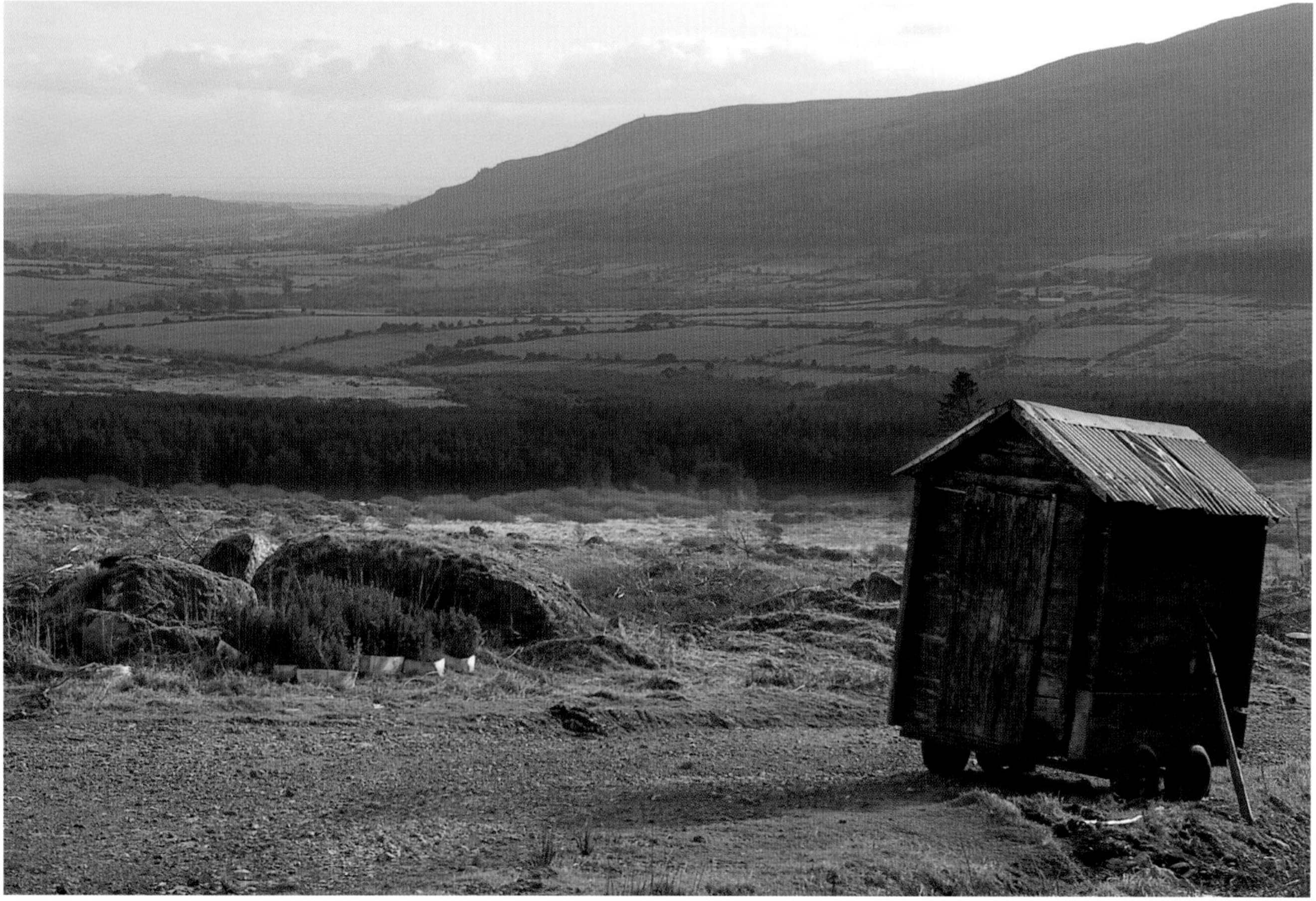

'Comeragh Retreat'

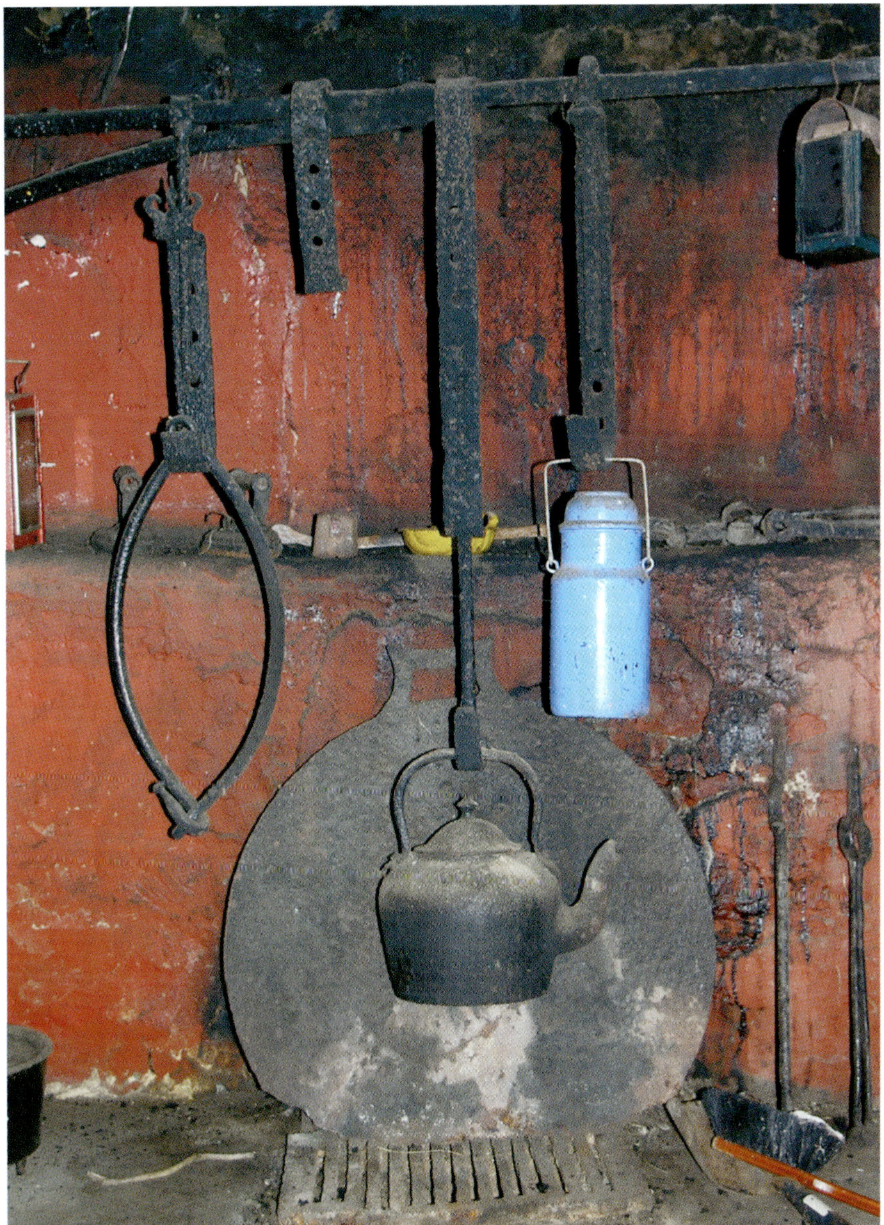

Lyre Heritage Centre

Summer Love

Summer, sunshine, the sea,
Laughter, love, you and me,
Walking along on the sand,
Smiles on our faces,
As we walk hand in hand.
Picnic at Kilmurrin Cove,
Blue skies high above,
Waves lapping on the beach,
Heaven is within our reach.

Summer, sunshine, the sea,
Laughter, love, you and me,
Drifting through a lovely summer's day,
You and I in a carefree way.
Swimming in the afternoon,
Soft waves on the beach play a gentle tune,
You say we'll always be as one,
I kiss your face caressed by summer sun.

The moon is shining high above,
I'm saying it's you I love,
Stars shining so bright,
I walk you home we kiss goodnight.
How happy we were on those summer days,
But that was before you went away,
Now there's nothing left for me to do,
Just walk this beach and think of you,
And summer, sunshine, the sea,
Laughter, love, you and me.

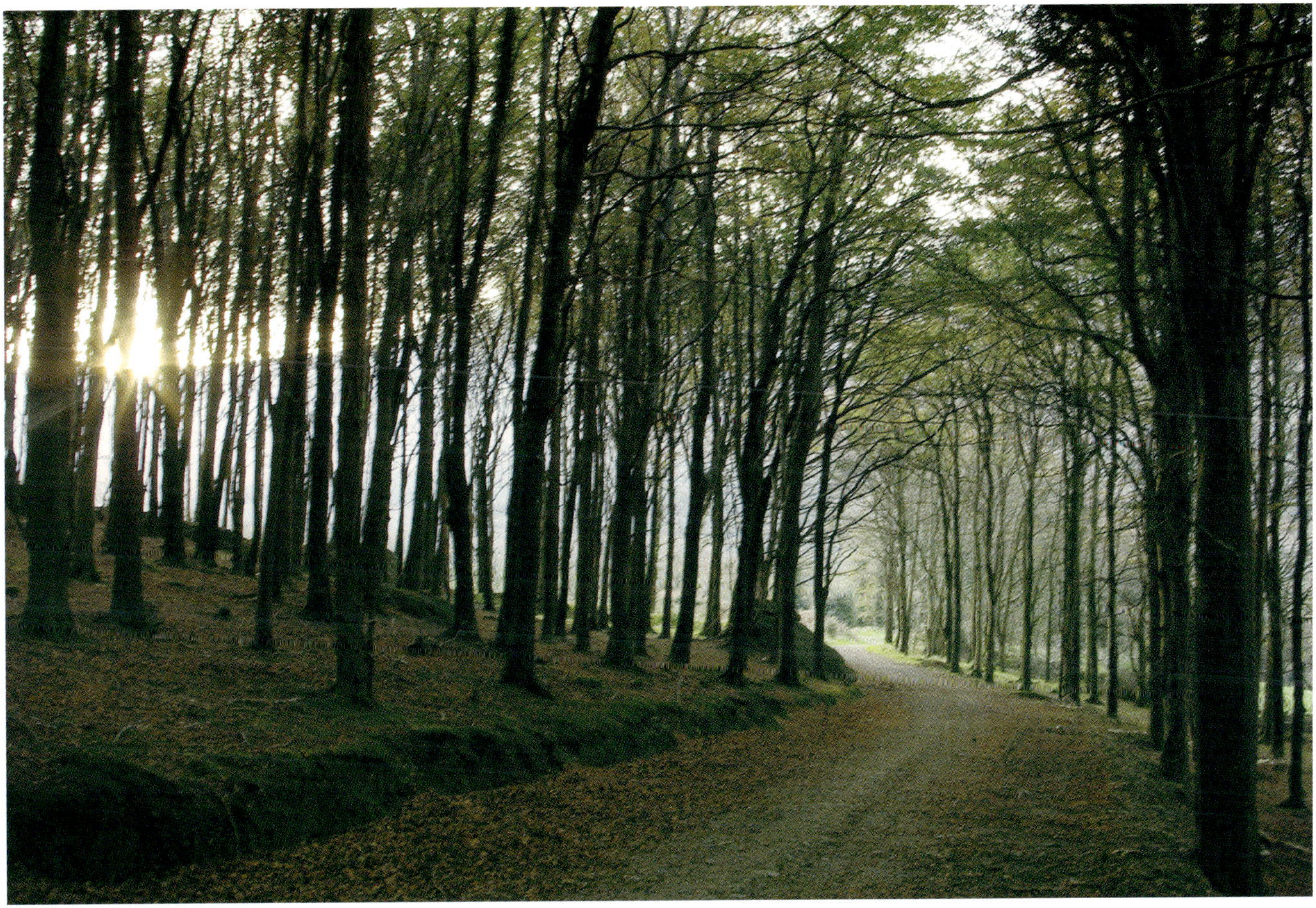

Forestry Track, Kilclooney

Winters Remembered

Grey north clouds roll dark across the sky,
This December day short, cold and dry,
I look out the door there's a flurry of white,
And I hear father say "we will have snow tonight."
Tonight all children will go happy to bed,
When they awake in the morning they know that instead,
Of an empty grey day and nowhere to go,
Their world will be filled with the magic of snow.

I go out to fetch some firewood and then,
I think to myself it's near Christmas again,
Soon we will go caroling through town,
Around us the snow will fall silently down.
Turning our world to a magical white,
Reflecting the starlight back into the night,
The lake it will turn to an arena of ice,
And we will go skating mid shrieks of delight.

We're out in the garden and talking of toys,
Making a snowman with coal for his eyes,
Grey winter days and long weary nights,
All are forgotten in this wonderful sight.
Snow on the ground, frost in the air,
We're all so happy now that Christmas is here;
If we smile in our sleep you know it's because
We're expecting a visit from old Santa Claus.

Early in the morning to pray we will go,
And give thanks to God because all people know,
That the babe in the manger kept warm by the hay,
Is the reason we have this wonderful day.
St Stephen's Day we'll go round with the wren and some holly,
Dancing and singing and really make jolly,
Anything you give us we'll gladly take,
If it's pennies or shillings or some Christmas cake.

And then when I'm older and cursing this snow,
Making my way from the glen down below,
With sheep that I have to bring in to their shack,
And I trudge through the drifts with one on my back.
My hands they are frozen, my face it is numb,
I think how I ever thought snow was such fun,
The birds have no food; they're too cold to sing,
And very old people are dreaming of spring.

They wonder how long this weather will last,
As they sit by the fire from winter's cold blast,
Then the laughter of children drifts by on the air,
Once more I remember those days without care.
When I was young and full of delight,
I ran and played in this magical white;
For a while I am back in those days long ago,
When happiness was Christmas, Santa and snow.

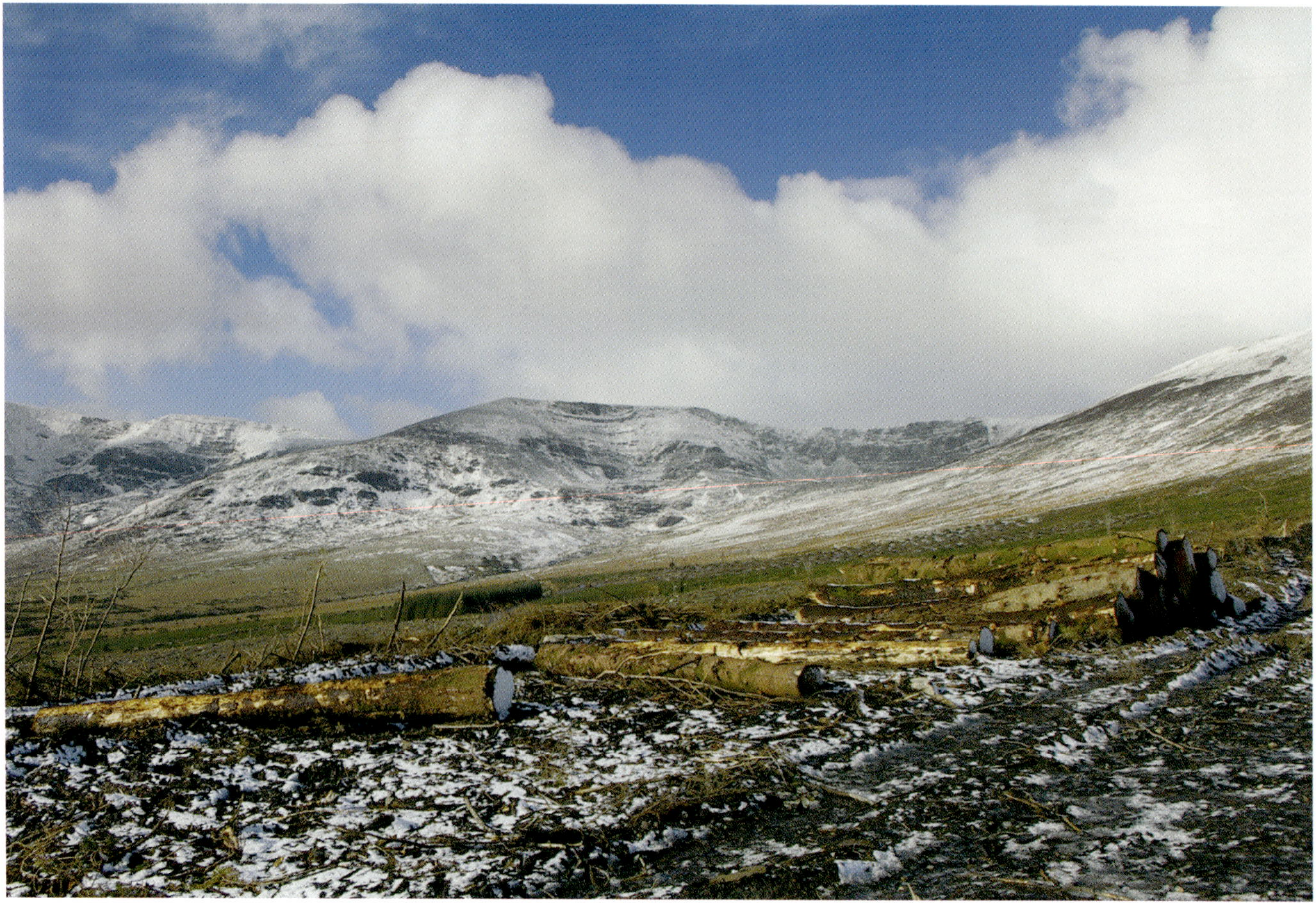

Comeragh Mountains

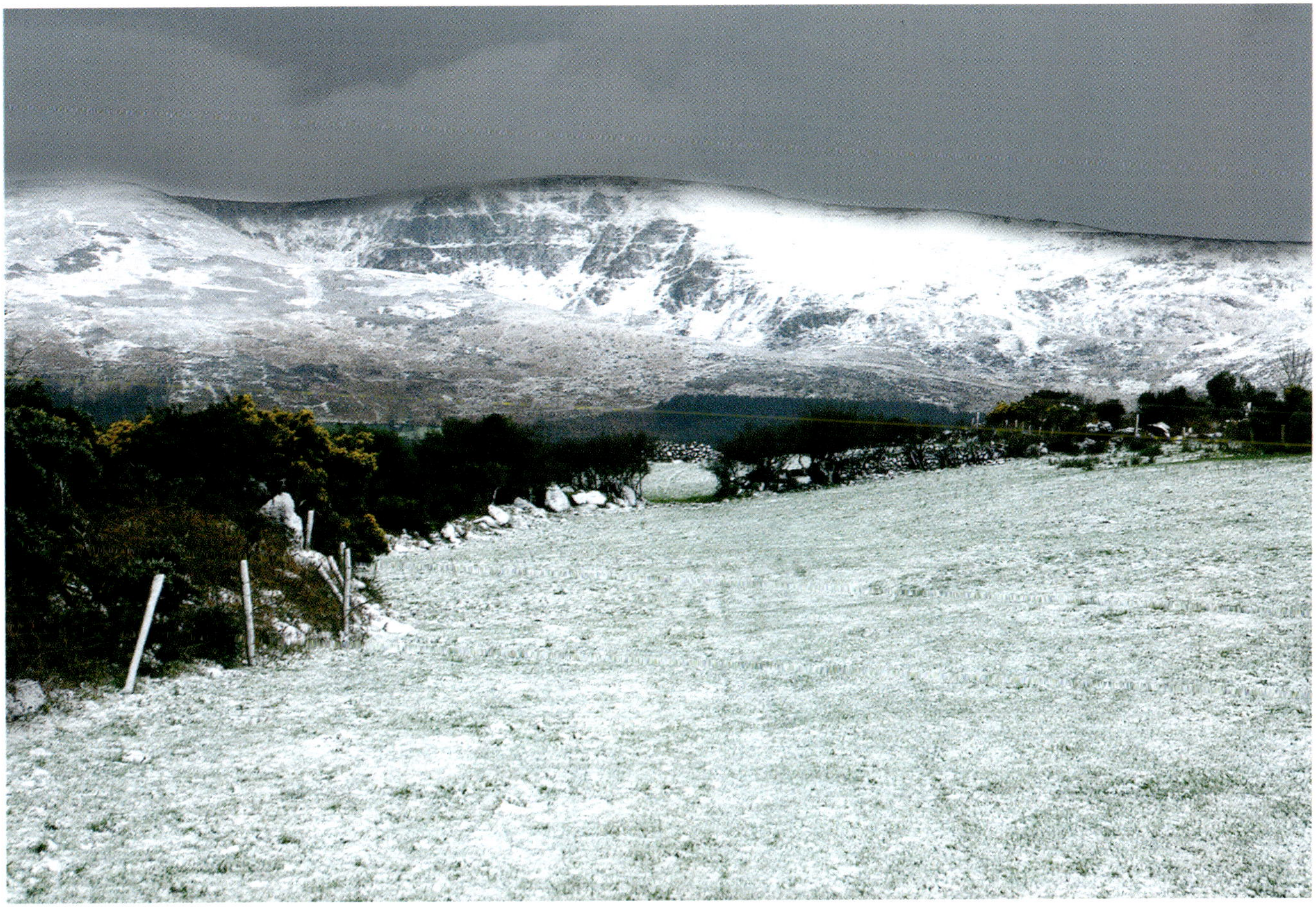

Comeragh Mountains

The Old Forge

He stood and looked around him, where the old forge used to be,
I walked down to meet him and that old man said to me:
"I remember that old forge, in the days of long ago,
From all around they'd gather here, and that old fire would glow,
I remember too the blacksmith, he was big and strong and tall,
As he hammered on the anvil, from his face the sweat would fall;
I still can hear the horses as they stamped upon the floor,
And all around the old forge yard stood half a dozen or more.

An old bag apron tied around him; in the fire he'd hold the shoe,
One hand upon the bellows, that fire was turning blue,
Then he'd take it to the anvil and hammer out its size,
As he tried it on the horse's hoof, you would hear a burning noise,
In from the field a man would come, with something broken from a plough,
"Do you think that you can mend it, I am waiting for it now",
Then someone with a harrow and how long will it take,
A shout from the yard, "did you make the iron for the gate?"

The forge it was a busy place, men would work and laugh and joke,
Above the thatch, year in, year out, would rise the blacksmith's smoke;
That forge was more to them than just a place of toil,
It was here they'd meet and share their news of truth and lies,
From here the news would travel of someone who passed away,
Or if a child was born at night that news was here next day;
It was many a game of football was played outside that door,
As all week long they caught and kicked, all last Sunday's score.

Down the road a common cart came noisily into sight,
Coming to the forge for a pair of bands fit secure and tight,
And sometimes in the winter when frost was in the air,
Some traveling men would come in and sit and be dry and warm there."
I had traveled with the old man, back down through the years,
I turned around to talk to him, but he had disappeared;
That old forge now has fallen, briars grow out from the wall,
And did I really see him that old man so big and strong and tall.

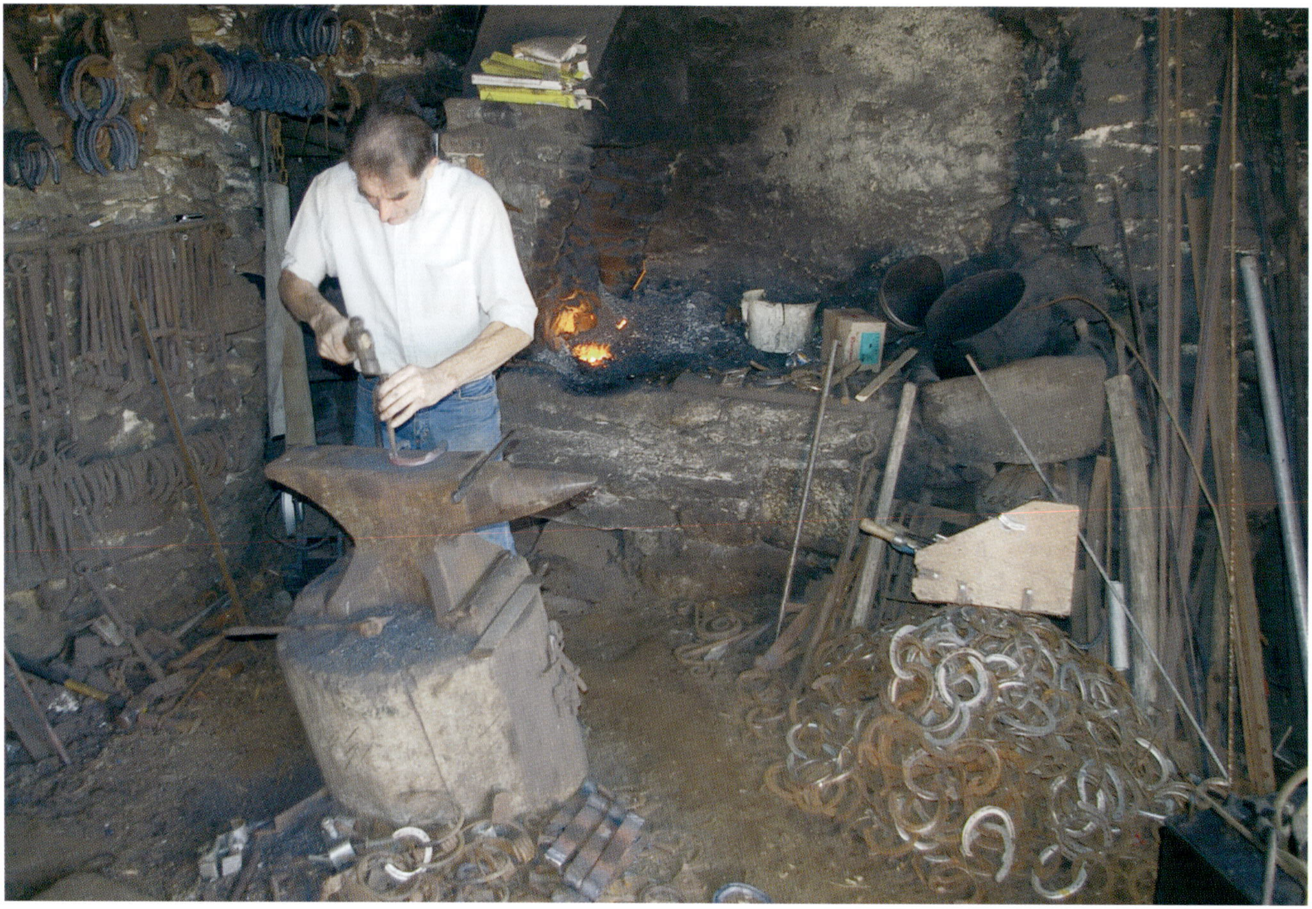

Farrier's Forge, Stradbally

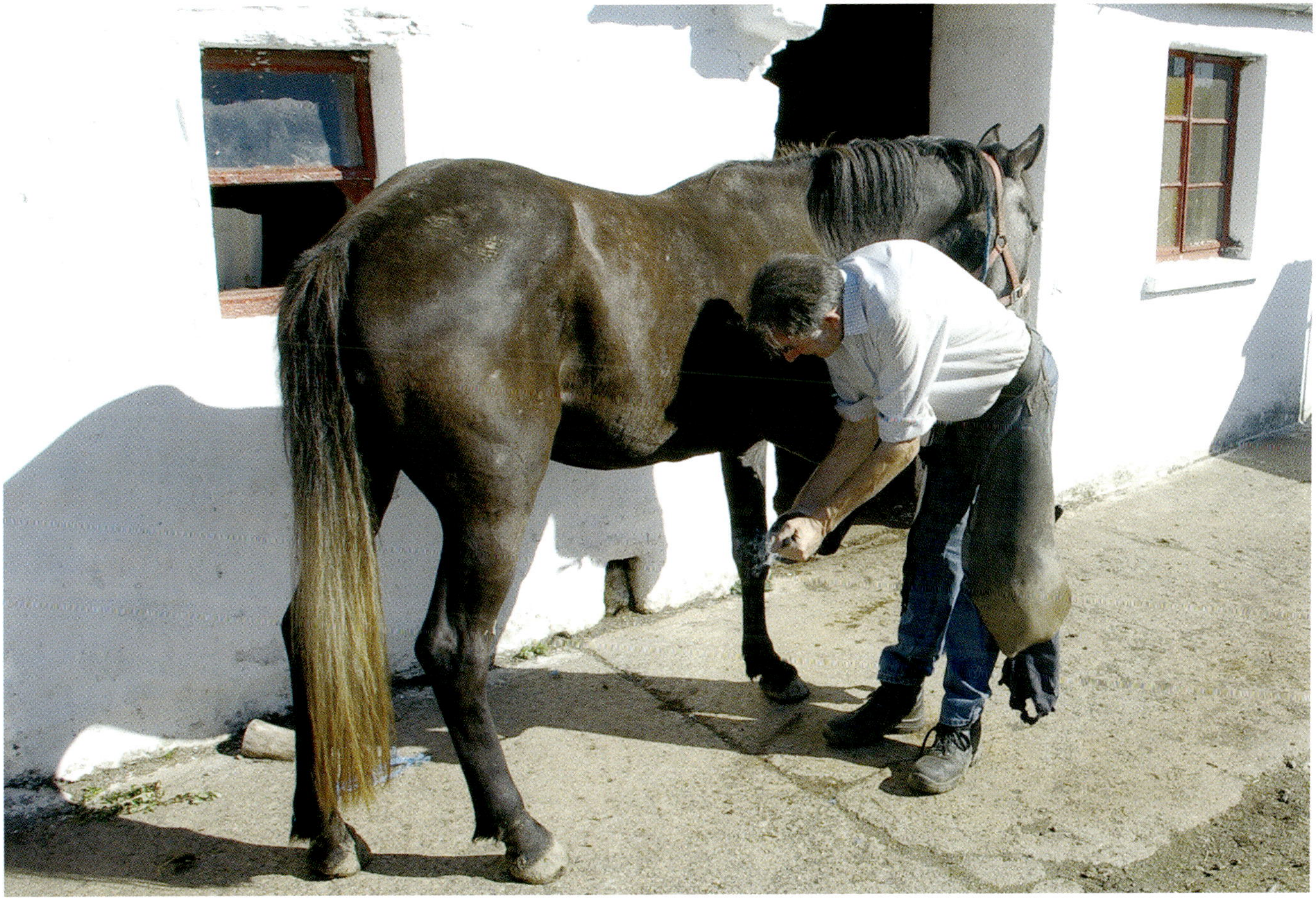

'New Shoes'

The Late Michael Power Memorial Swim

Kilmurrin Cove on Christmas Day, sure everyone was there,
For the Michael Power Memorial Swim they came from everywhere.
They came from Waterford City, Clonmel and Carrick too,
From Kill, Dunhill, Bonmahon the swim they came to do.
From Kilmac', Carroll's Cross and Newtown and also from Tramore,
A mighty crowd assembled on Kilmurrin's stony shore,
The sun was shining nicely; the waves broke on the sand,
One hundred and thirty swimmers I counted on the strand.
The swimmers charged the water, you should hear them cheer and shout.
They dived and splashed and dived again, then came shivering out.

The spectators on the shoreline cheered them all the way,
Everyone enjoyed themselves on this lovely Christmas Day.
Lifeguards from Bonmahon saw it safely through,
We are glad you came and we say thanks to you.
Maureen Kirwan and Lily Doody supplied punch for one and all,
The swimmers were really grateful; the measures were far from small.
A speech from Martin Kiely, he is the mayor of Kill,
A speech to him comes easy; the man has words at will.
Bovril and hot soup clutched in the children's hand,
And a happy Christmas to you, God my shoes are full of sand!

Michael Power had an idea back in nineteen eighty-two,
Said he was going to swim all the winter through.
He got some friends to join him in nineteen eight-three,
And that was the first swim they did for charity.
In nineteen eighty-four on a cold December day,
Suddenly and peacefully Michael Power passed away.
A shocked crowd gathered for the Christmas swim.
It was Michael who started it so they named it after him.
The waves are quietly breaking at Kilmurrin's lovely cove,
Michael I hope you are watching from your home above.

As you watch the swimmers and the very large crowd,
You must be smiling quietly and feeling very proud.
For the crowd that's gathered here is gathered in your name,
And you are saying "thank you, I am glad you came."
We are proud to be here, to help the needy and the sick,
What's ten minutes in the water? It's over very quick.
By swimming you are helping someone less fortunate than you,
Some deserving cause we will give the money to.
Please God next year we will see you in Kilmurrin by the sea,
For the Michael Power Memorial Swim, its all for charity.

The seagulls are flying high up in the sky,
Alone in Kilmurrin I hear their loud cry;
White horses are rolling in from the blue,
As I walk this quiet cove I am thinking of you.
In a vision I see you walking the strand,
A towel on your shoulder, togs in your hand,
As you came nearer you ask what it is like,
Above in the car park I can see your old bike,
A crash from a wave and the vision is gone,
St. Stephen's Day in Kilmurrin alone I walk on.

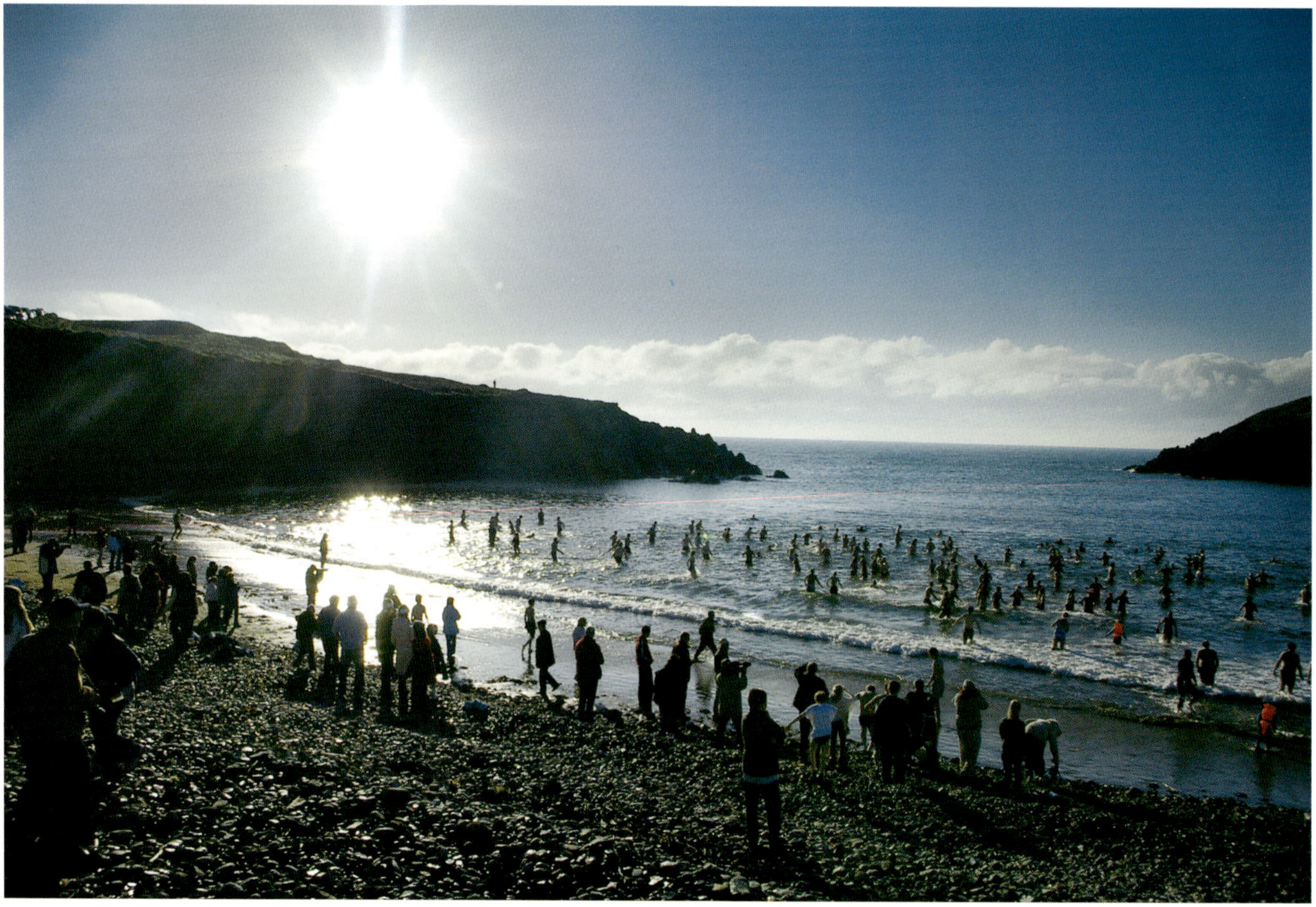

Christmas Day Swim, Kilmurrin Cove

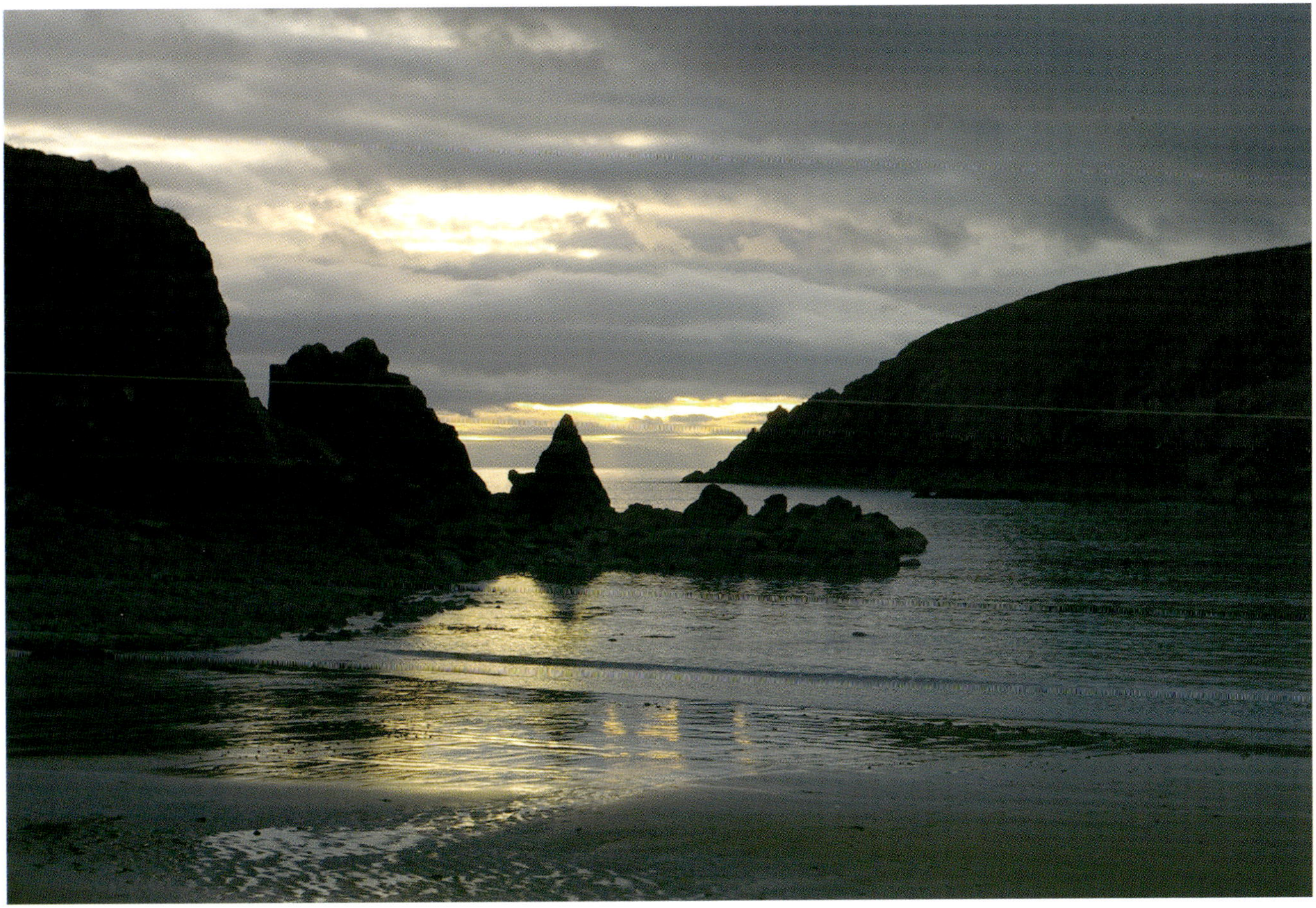

Kilmurrin Cove

On a Visit to Coumshingaun

Halfway through my climb I stopped for a rest,
And looked up at the mountain,
A grey mist crept slowly down from the summit,
And as I continued up, the mist descended down the steep cliff,
Across the surface of the lake and up the other side,
As I arrived at my destination it engulfed me,
And obscured what I had come to view,
Then slowly the mist moved down the mountain,
And evaporated in the valley below;
Its departure revealed to me the cold water of Coumshingaun,
I stood in silence and admired the beauteous solitude,
The wondrous wildness of this place stunned me,
Then I turned and looked down on the valley stretching away to the sea,
Shadows of the passing clouds sailed ghostlike,
Across a colourful patchwork of fields,
And I gazed in awe;
I closed my eyes and inhaled deep the crisp mountain air,
It was as if I had become part of the mountain and the mountain part of me.

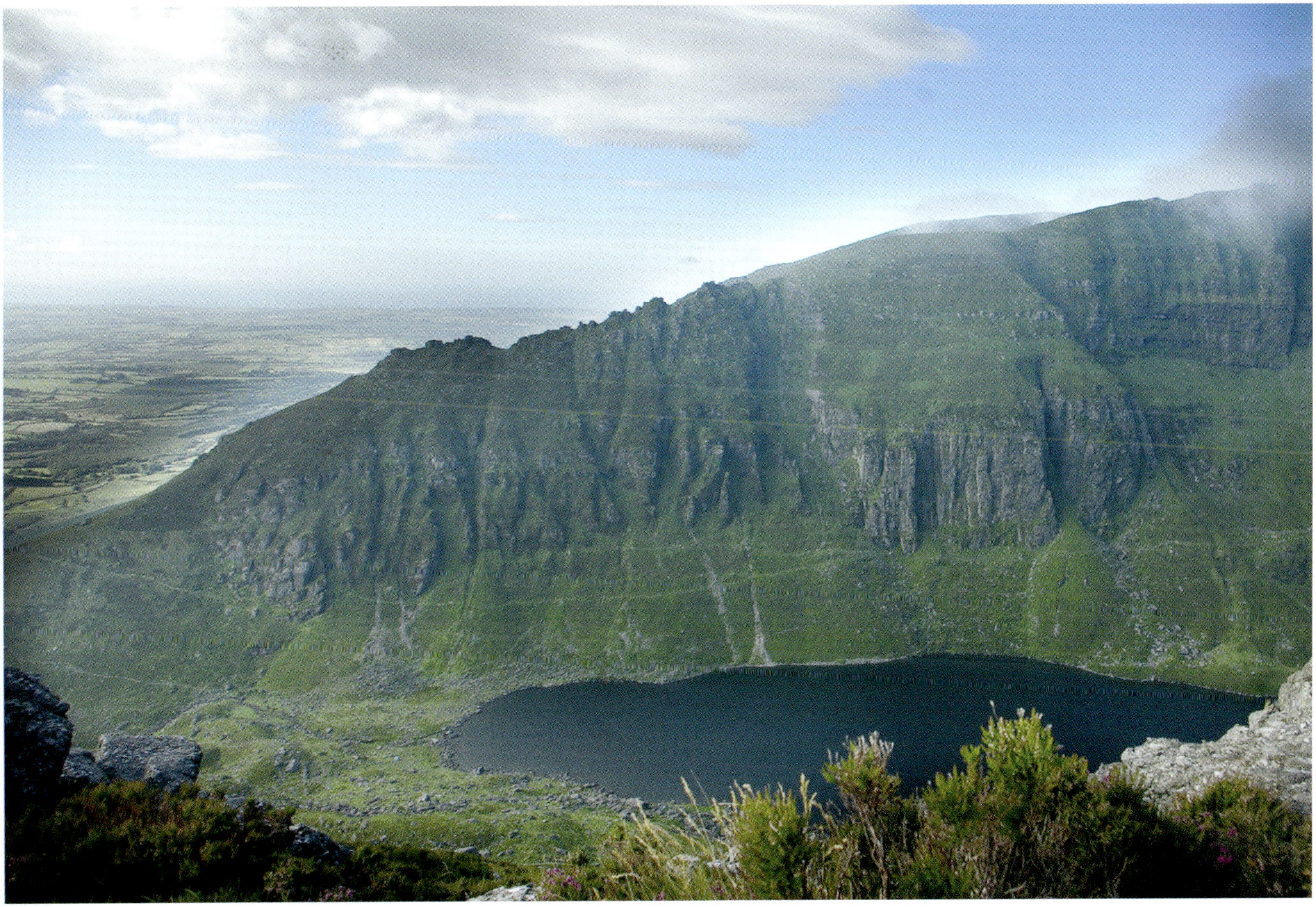

Coumshingaun, Comeragh Mountains

Thank You, Co. Council

I was sitting at the table enjoying my cup of tea,
When the lads ran in and said "Daddy come and see!"
They really were excited, amazement in their eyes,
Had a spaceship landed with aliens from the skies?
I ran out to the garden and jumped over the gate,
I landed in a pothole; well it really was a lake.
Now, you know I cannot swim, but I was quick to learn,
To avoid the jaws of a crocodile, I grabbed a ten foot fern;
I climbed up to the side and on the ground I tumbled,
Lost in a strange world, an Irish roadside jungle.

I detoured around the pothole and fought my way back,
In the briars and weeds, now and then, a twig would crack;
Was it an elephant, a vicious tiger or lion?
Maybe a cannibal and his dinner frying?
Within the hour I was home, my clothes torn and tattered,
I was wet and miserable, my teeth began to chatter;
The lads said "Daddy, can you hear it? It's getting very near."
To get a better view, I climbed upon the pier;
With my hands up to my eyes I did some jungle gazing,
And believe me what I saw, it really was amazing.

Coming down the road with a clatter and clutter,
I know it's hard to believe, it was the Council roadside cutter;
For weeks we were cut off, but we never gave up hope,
We were always sending signals, we had plenty weeds for smoke.
Now we are going to be saved, help is on the way,
Let us cheer the Council once more, they've saved the day;
But could they have come sooner, did we have to wait so long?
We are in August, once more the summer's gone;
This three mile stretch of road, from Kilmurrin up to Kill,
You must be brave to travel it, or lost the will to live.

But it has its consolations, the wild flowers are very quaint,
Some with natural colours and some with metallic paint;
There are blue and red and yellow, all pleasing to the eye,
All taken from the side of the cars as they go driving by.
Where is all the money that the motorist pays in taxes?
I think I'll change my insurance to third party, fire and scratches;
That tax disc is expensive and you must keep it on display,
But I will only tax the car from September up to May;
Then I'll park and lock it, and oil up my rusty bike,
And I will cycle down the road, two feet between the dykes.

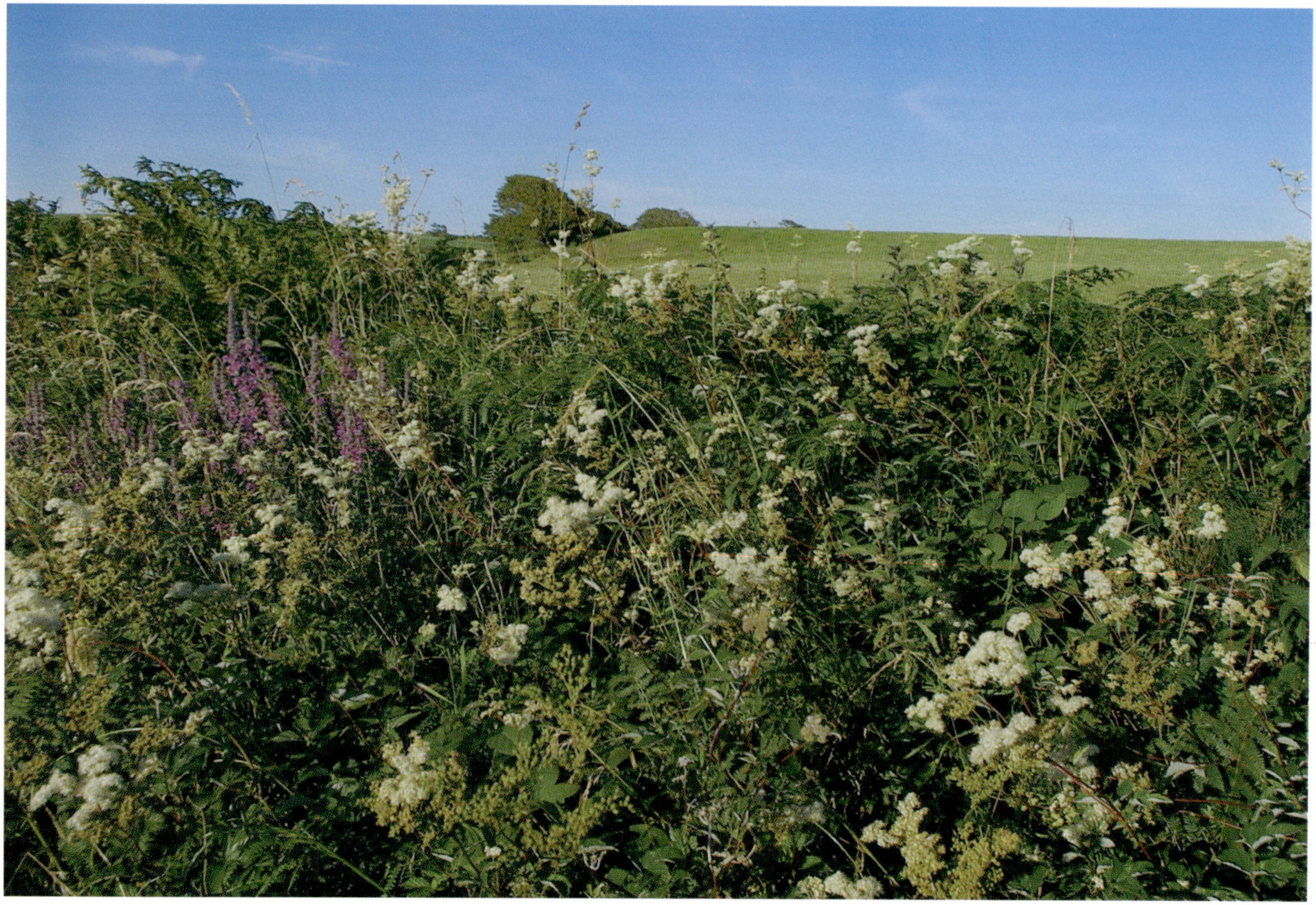

Hedgerow, Kilmurrin

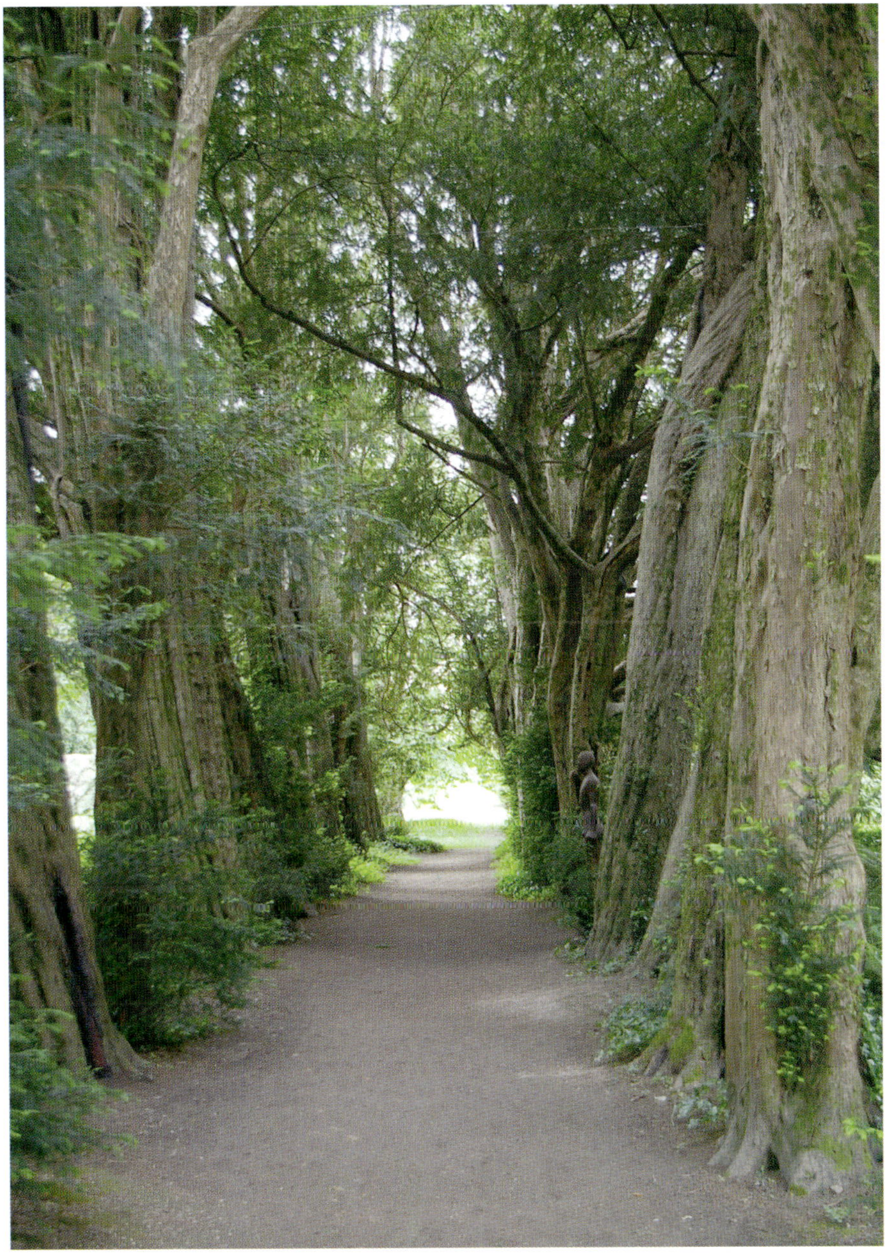

Lismore Castle Gardens

Blessing of the Boats at Boatstrand

A full tide lapping against the dock wall,
Boats mirrored in the water, some big, some small,
The sea is shimmering in the summer sun,
Out on the horizon, sky and ocean merge into one,
Nets and pots are stacked along the dock,
Old boats now abandoned and left to rot.

Seagulls circling in the July air,
Beside a makeshift alter a group kneels in prayer,
Stubborn candles refuse to light in the summer breeze,
A wind surfer glides along with peaceful ease,
A quick twist of a sail he turns for shore,
And joins with the crowd 'til mass is o'er.

Fresh flowers in vases on the alter stand,
And two more bunches are on the sand,
Older people bring a seat so they can sit,
Remembering when they came here young and fit,
Small children playing in the sand,
The Host held high in Father Condon's hand.

Fishermen, young and old, are gathered here,
To ask God's protection for another year;
The priest asks God to guide us on our way,
Protect all who go to sea, to work or play;
Salt and water mixed and prayers are said,
In the name of trinity the waters spread.

Father Condon walks out along the wall,
"Please bless these boats", to God he calls,
Holy water filled in bottles to take away,
To spread at home another day;
Mass now over the people stand and chat,
Please God next year we will all be back.

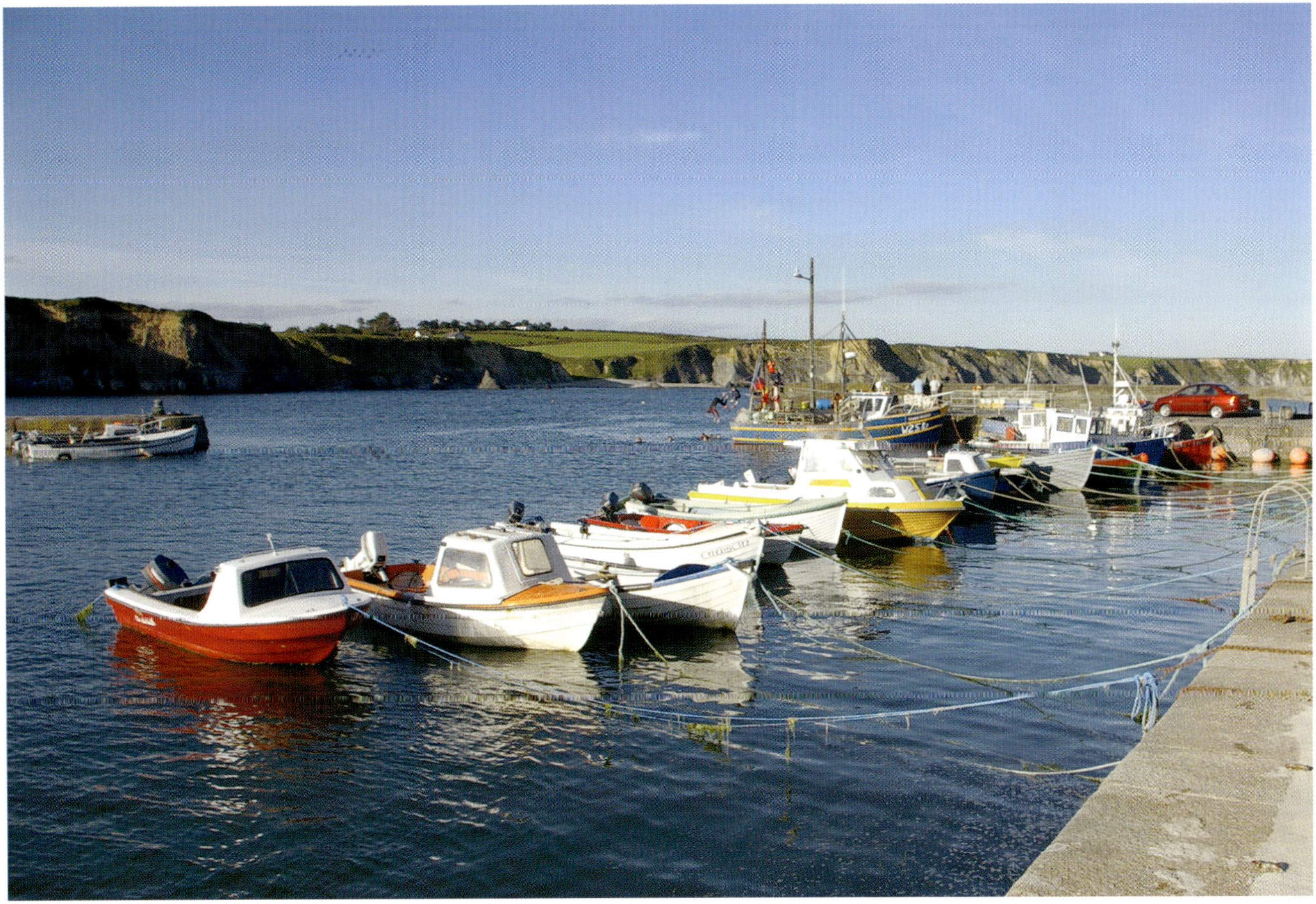

Boatstrand

Wonderful Waterford

Crystal clear streams, that flow toward the ocean,
Golden cornfields the wind sets in motion,
Peaceful green valleys, the birds' lovely song,
And to the mountains for walks I have gone.
Swimming in summer, winter cold snow,
This is my home, the place that I know,
The colours of autumn, the blossom of spring,
Always and ever your praises I'll sing.

Wonderful Waterford my home so fair,
Smiling faces and people who care,
Rivers and valleys, mountains and sea,
City or county its heaven to me,
Beautiful scenery, a friendly hello,
Wonderful Waterford, I love you so.

Buses and cars clog up every street,
Pavements are worn from pounding of feet,
People are busy from morning to night,
Walking and talking, but that's city life.
Big city bars where you can meet,
Quaint little cafés and food there to eat,
The hustle and bustle of the city for me,
This is my life and it always will be.

The primrose in spring a grand sight to see,
The lights of the city are heaven to me,
A quiet country road at the end of the day,
Cinemas, night clubs, or go see a play,
To go strolling along the bank of a stream,
A night on the town with the one of your dreams.
The lovely fresh scent of a forest of pine,
And the eight thirty bus arriving at nine.

Wonderful Waterford my home so fair,
Smiling faces and people who care,
Rivers and valleys, mountains and sea,
City or county its heaven to me,
Beautiful scenery, a friendly hello,
Wonderful Waterford, I love you so.

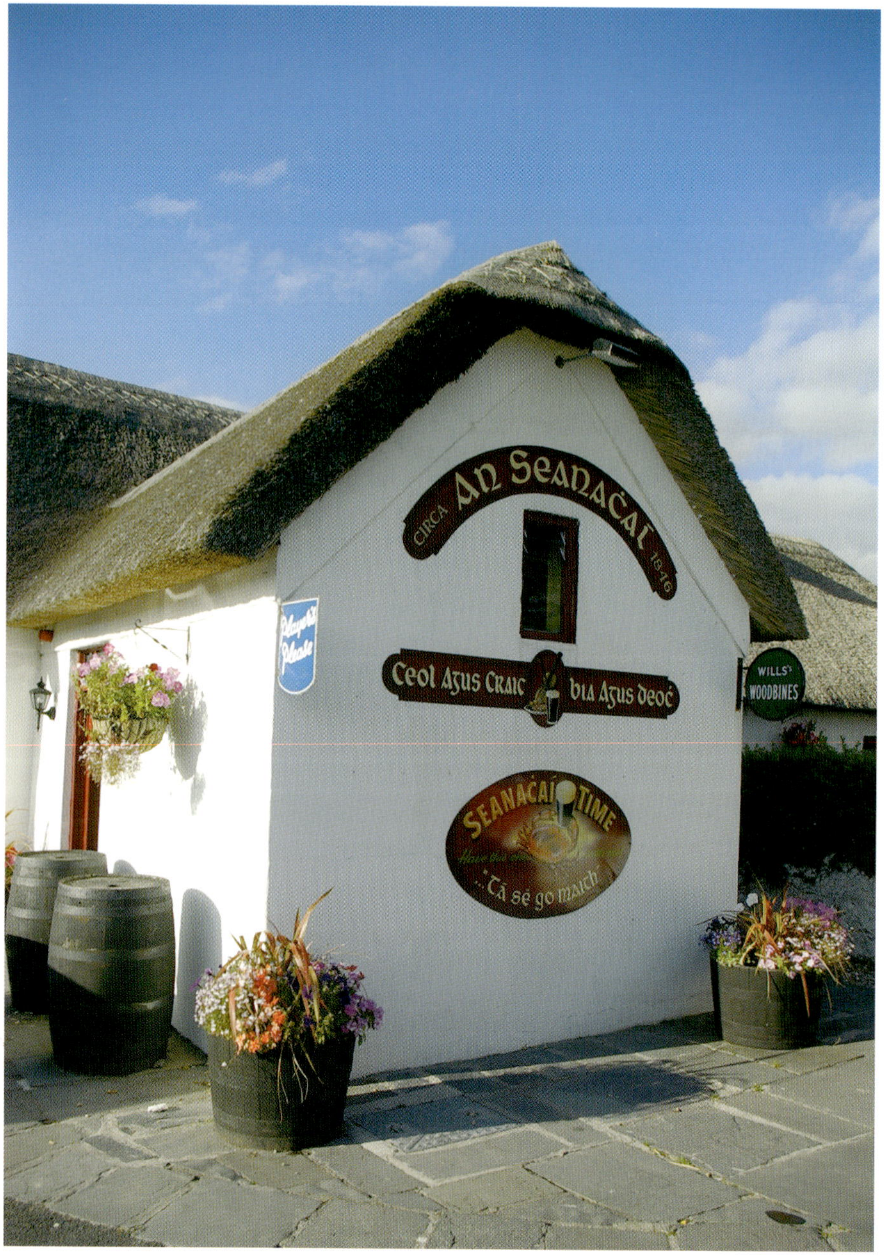

An Seanachai Pub, Ring

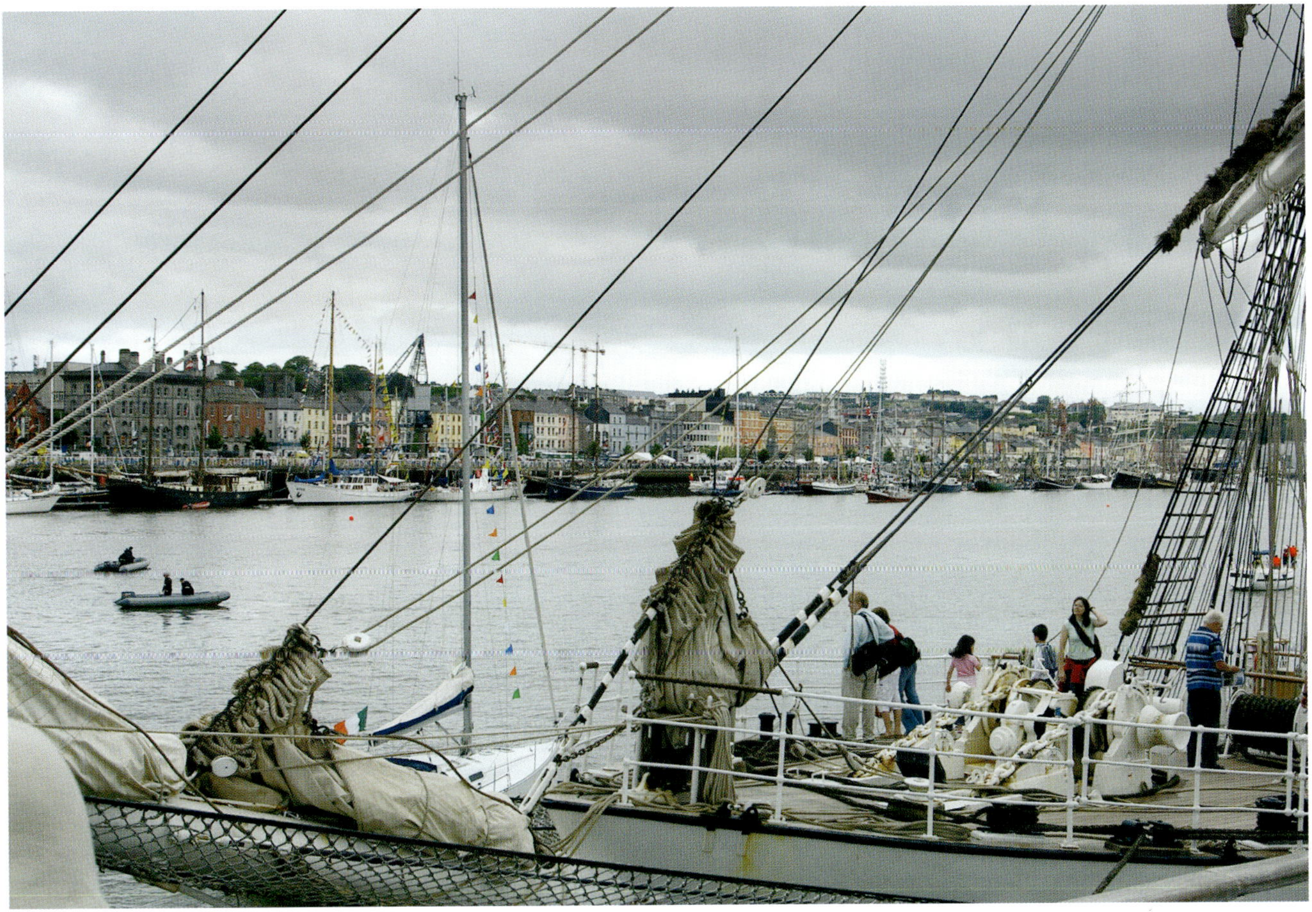

The Tall Ships 2005, Waterford City

The Old Blessed Well

There's a cure in the old blessed well,
That's what the old people tell,
Between dusk and dawn is the time to go there,
Kneel by the well and offer a prayer,
To St. Ita or St. Bernard, you make your choice,
A prayer to both would be my advice.

Out of the well flows a stream to the west,
Dip in a cloth for the water is blest,
Rub on the water and make the sign of the cross,
Now hang the cloth on the nearby old sceach,
Visit twice more and you can rest assured,
Any ailment you have will surely be cured.

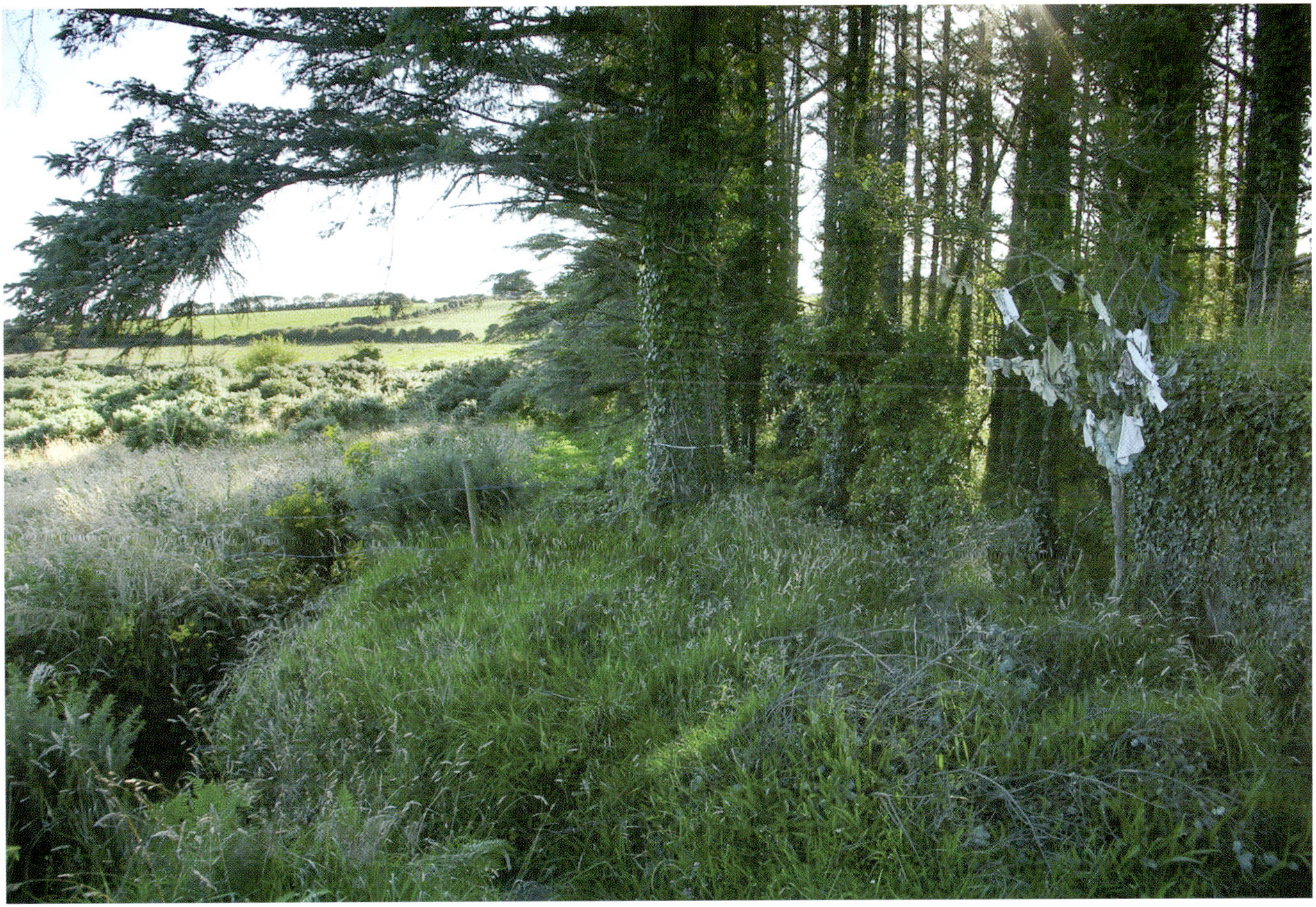

St Ita's / St Bernard's Well, Kill

Together

Where the land meets the ocean and so ends our walk,
We will sit by the shoreline and there we will talk;
Our clothes we'll take off and we will jump in,
So happy together, we will go for a swim.
At one with nature in the home of the fish,
We'll touch each other and tenderly kiss;
When we emerge from the ocean, your hand in mine,
We will lie on the sand and rest for awhile.
No clouds in the sky, the sun high above,
On a quiet beach in Waterford, we will make love;
As we lie together our bodies entwined,
We know these moments of pleasure will last a lifetime.
We will walk together life's unpredictable road,
Sharing life's pleasures and sharing life's load;
And when we are older, we will think of our youth,
Spent searching for pleasure and seeking the truth.
Tomorrow will come but what will it bring?
In the darkness of winter, we will think of the spring.

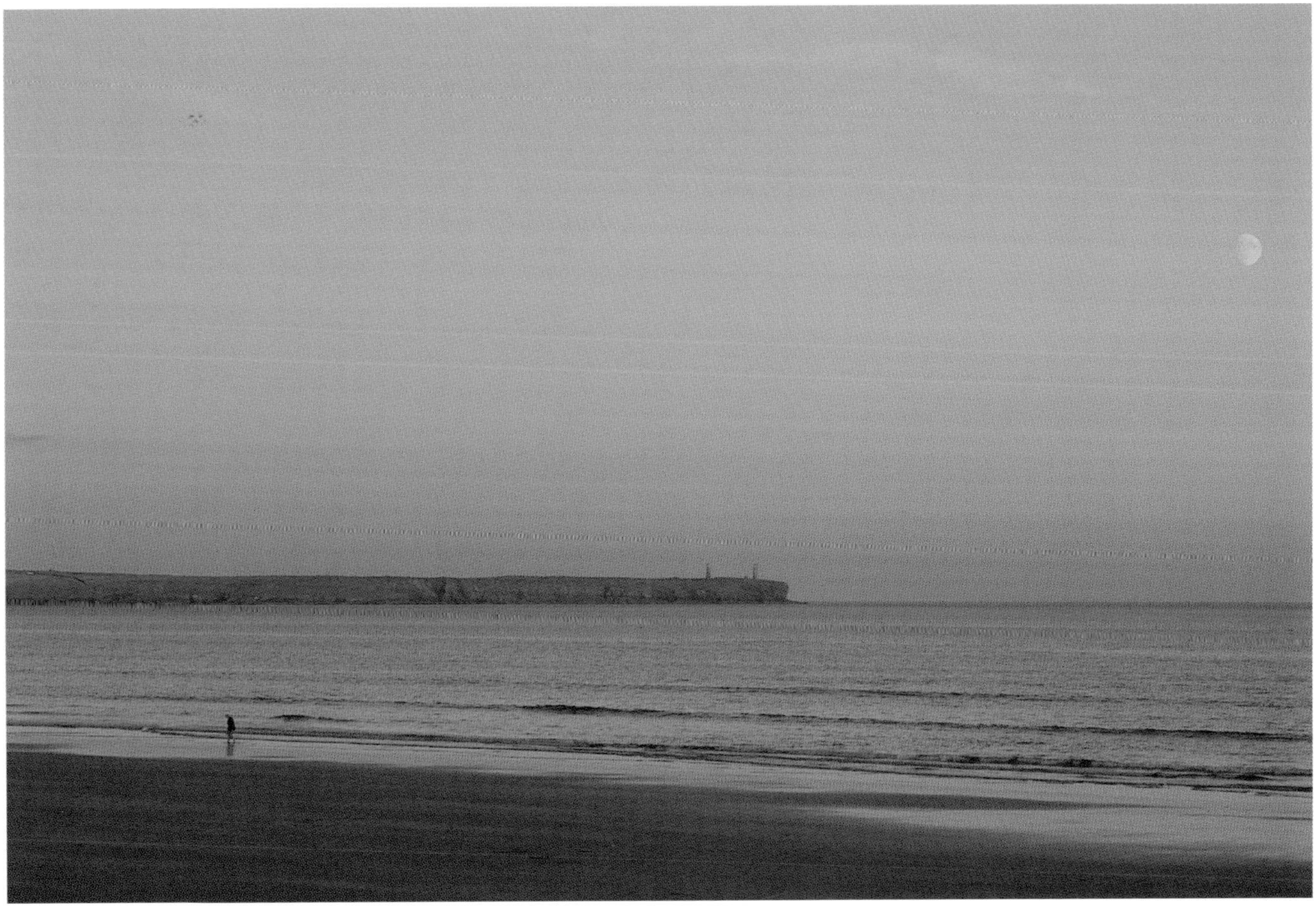

Tramore

Free Spirit

Do not look for me in a quiet graveyard, for I am not within,
When the leaves rustle on the tree, that is me;
I am the wind on the mountain,
The laughing brook in the green valley,
And I am also the sea spray on your face.

Do not grieve for me, rejoice, for I am free,
I have shaken off the shackles of my earthly existence;
I can be what I want and travel at will,
I will surf the cornfields in summer,
And in winter dance with the northern lights.

I am the wisp of white cloud floating over the flowers of spring,
And I drift with the autumn mist,
Sometime in the future you too will cease your earthly existence,
And you will join with me and together forever,
We will travel the never ending universe.

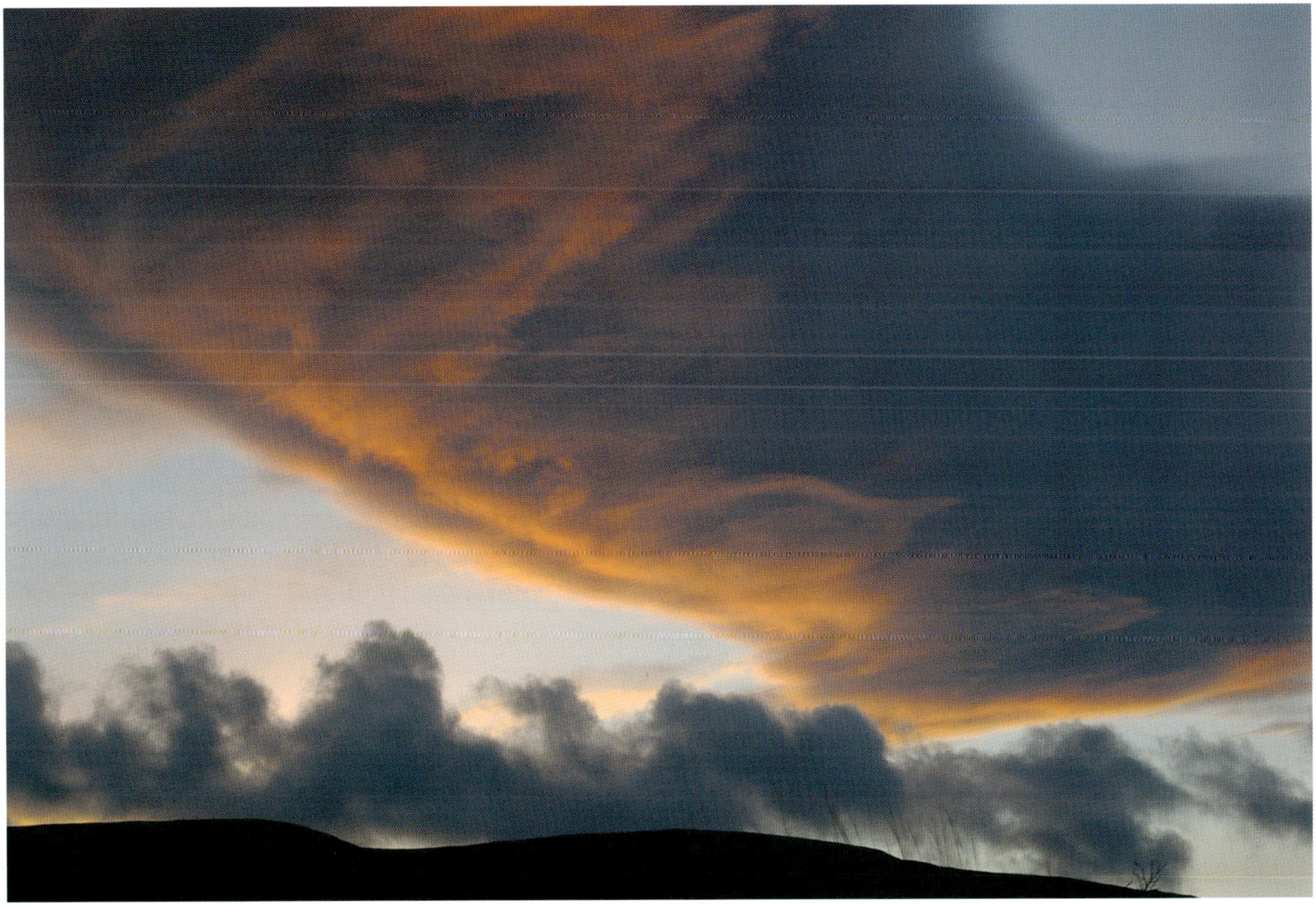

'Autumn Blaze', Comeragh Mountains

Biographies

Jackie Elger

Fiantas Photography
Kilrossanty
Co. Waterford
Ireland
Tel: 086 1760280
Email: jackie@fiantas.com
Web: www.fiantas.com

Jackie Elger, (nee McCarthy), is a freelance photographer based in Co. Waterford. Her work focuses on capturing the wild beauty of the Irish landscape and its heritage.

Jackie was born in Dublin and lived there until she was sixteen, when the family returned to their native Co. Clare. After completing her secondary education she moved to Oxfordshire, England, where she obtained a degree in Environmental Science from the Open University. Jackie worked as a laboratory technician in the Physical Chemistry Laboratory of Oxford University for twelve years. It was here that she began to develop her interest in photography through access to the laboratory's darkroom and printing facilities.

Jackie returned to Ireland in 2003, settling in the foothills of the Comeragh Mountains, with her husband Peter and their two children. She set up Fiántas Photography as a way of commercialising her passion for landscape and macro photography. She continues to grow this business by exhibiting her work; writing for community magazines and selling her prints and cards through local retailers. She has also gained a diploma in Photography from The Regent Academy of Fine Arts, London.

Tom Power

Poet and writer, Tom Power, a native of Co. Waterford, lives in the parish of Kill, with his wife Hannah and three children. Tom has been writing poems for many years. Some have been published in magazines and newspapers and read out on radio stations such as R.T.E. and W.L.R. He has also written two one act plays, which were performed to acclaim at the Gaelach Gorm theatre in Kill. Tom has also written several short stories and some of his songs have been recorded by local musicians. He is at present working on a fiction book which he hopes to publish shortly.